Contemporary
Paper-Pieced Quilts

by Jeannie Jenkins

Contemporary
Paper-Pieced Quilts
by Jeannie Jenkins

Landauer Publishing (*www.landauerpub.com*) is an imprint of Fox Chapel Publishing Company, Inc.

Copyright © 2018 by Jeannie Jenkins and Fox Chapel Publishing Company, Inc. 903 Square Street, Mount Joy, PA 17552.

Project Team:
Vice President-Content: Christopher Reggio
Editor: Laurel Albright/Sue Voegtlin
Designer: Laurel Albright
Photographer: Sue Voegtlin

ISBN 13: 978-1-947163-02-7

The Cataloging-in-Publication Data is on file with the Library of Congress.

We are always looking for talented authors. To submit an idea, please send a brief inquiry to acquisitions@ foxchapelpublishing.com.

Printed in Singapore

21 20 19 18   2 4 6 8 10 9 7 5 3 1

This book has been published with the intent to provide accurate and authoritative information in regard to the subject matter within. While every precaution has been taken in the preparation of this book, the author and publisher expressly disclaim any responsibility for any errors, omissions, or adverse effects arising from the use or application of the information contained herein.

Contents

Introduction

One of my favorite blocks of all time is the star block from the Supernova quilt. I love that the star has 45 and 60 degree angles that create a curved appearance without needing to sew a curved seam. But I struggled with accuracy on this block. Sewing a long bias seam was daunting and it usually ended up in frustration and disappointment.

Then I found if I used a paper piecing method I could make a block without swearing! In fact, I loved the process; no distortion, points were sharp, and bias edge blocks matched when assembled. Who could ask for more?

About The Author

Award winning quilt maker, long arm quilter, designer, and teacher, Jeannie's work has been published in magazines and displayed worldwide. She is the third generation in her family to graduate from O.C.A.D. (Ontario College of Art and Design) and was raised around art! She began sewing as a child and took a dressmaking course at the age of 10. That was the beginning of her love of sewing, making most of her clothes as a teenager.

Jeannie dabbled in quilting in 1979 when a friend commissioned her to make two quilts. It was before rotary cutters and other time saving tools, and the fabrics were less than inspiring. After a few commissions her interest waned, so she took a break for a number of years.

After graduating from college, Jeannie taught Arts and Crafts to seniors for the Toronto Board of Education. When one of the women in her class took her to a quilt guild meeting in 1990 it re-introduced her to quilting. The industry had changed and fabrics had improved. This began her journey into quilt making and she has never looked back.

Between starting a family, working and teaching in various quilt shops, Jeannie's passion is just as strong today as it was in 1990. She loves sharing her passion with other quilters.

Jeannie lives in Toronto Ontario, Canada with her husband, two grown kids, their cat and two dogs.

Dedication

Thank you so much to all my family for all of their love and support. To my husband Bruce, who has always supported my creativity. I am sure he is grateful that I have been way too busy to haul home any curb side finds for future D.I.Y.'s. To my kids, Katie and Billy who have been born into my quilting world. They are the light of my life. I have loved watching you grow into beautiful (inside and out) young adults that I am very proud of. To my mom who shared her artistic ability with me, and to my dad who has always been very supportive of me.

Acknowledgments

To my friends, you know who you are. I am so lucky to have all of you in my life! You have been there in good times and bad. To Shirley Dawson who messaged me many words of encouragement during this process and her expertise and piecing help on "Guess How Much I Love You" quilt. And to Samarra Khaja who lit this path for me at a time of transition. What started as a business relationship blossomed into a valued friendship.

Resources

- Hoffman Fabrics; *www.hoffmanfabrics.com*
- Robert Kaufman; *www.robertkaufman.com*
- Lecien; *www.lecien.co.jp*
- The Warm Company; *www.warmcompany.com*
- Daylight Company; *www.daylightcompany.com*
- Samarra Khaja; *www.samarrakhaja.com*
- Alison Glass; *www.alisonglass.com*
- Janome; *www.janome.com*

Paper Piecing 101

Tools & Supplies

The sewing notions shown below can help make your paper piecing experience easier and you may already have some of these tools in your sewing space. The light box, for instance, can easily be replaced using an exterior window to trace a pattern. Your finger can press a seam open as easily as a wooden seam roller. Once you get started, you'll decide which tools are your favorites and which ones work best for you.

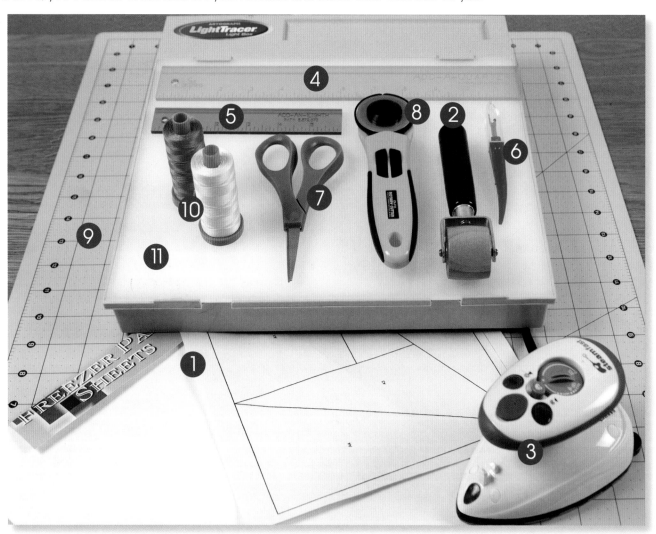

1. Foundation Paper Piecing paper (I like Carol Doak's foundation paper), freezer paper, and office copy paper

2. Wooden Seam Roller

3. Iron

4. Add-A-Quarter® ruler

5. Add-An-Eighth™ ruler

6. Seam Ripper

7. Paper Scissors

8. Rotary Cutter

9. Cutting Mat

10. Neutral Thread

11. Light Box

The Patterns

Paper piecing uses a pattern on paper, not unlike a garment sewing pattern. Within the pattern are "templates" for the shapes of fabric you'll cut to make a block. Some patterns are made up of "segments" that are pieced and then sewn together to complete a block and numbers and letters guide you as you sew the fabric shapes together.

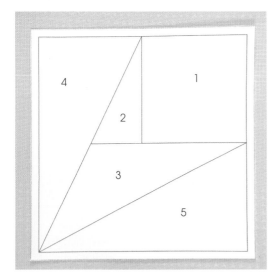

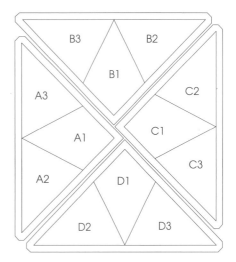

The front of the paper pattern has sewing and seam lines, numbers, and letters. Just like a paint-by-number picture, number 1 is the starting point. Add and pin fabric shapes to the back of the pattern and continue adding and sewing in numerical order.

The pattern above is made up of four segments. Numbers will include a letter starting with "A". Each segment is sewn individually and segments are sewn together in alphabetical order A-B, C-D, and then sewn together matching the center seam to complete the block.

Patterns in this book need to be enlarged. Instructions for each project will tell you how many copies to make of each pattern. The number includes an extra to use as a pattern when cutting fabric shapes.

Enlarge a pattern on regular office copy paper. Use this as the master copy to print on foundation or freezer paper. (See page 8) This master will ensure that all additional copies of patterns are accurate. The 1/4" (0.635cm) seam allowance on all sides need to remain a part of the pattern. When your block is finished, this becomes the trim line to square up your block. It's also the seam allowance as you sew blocks together.

Adjust the stitch length on your sewing machine so that the stitches are small enough to weaken the paper but long enough to "un-sew" a seam if it is sewn wrong. I suggest 15-16 stitches per inch.

Paper piecing is worked from the back to the front of a paper pattern, which may seem confusing. But once you've made a few blocks it becomes easier! Fabric shapes are centered and pinned on the back of the pattern, (the plain side), and then sewn on the lines on the front of the pattern. When the paper is removed, the seam lines are revealed. Flip to the front to see a perfectly pieced block!

Fabric requirements include the extra needed to leave a 1/2" (1.27cm) around all sides of the fabric shapes. The cut can be "rough" meaning it doesn't need to be exact. This seems like alot but once you become familiar with the paper piecing technique, you can reduce the cut size to a minimum of 3/8" (0.952) on all sides of your fabric shape. After you have completed your project, use any extra fabric to add some interest to your backing piece or save for a scrappy project.

Using Patterns to Cut Shapes

When you start a project, you will be cutting multiple fabric pieces for the shapes in the blocks.

It's a good idea to make a single fabric pattern, check to make sure it overlaps the sewing lines on the paper pattern, and then cut all other pieces, knowing they will be the correct size. If you are using foundation paper, unpin the paper and use this paper shape to cut the rest of your fabric.

The same technique applies if you are using freezer paper but there is no need to remove it from the fabric shape since it is ironed on. Use this paper and fabric shape to cut out the rest of your fabric shapes.

NOTE: *Whether you use foundation paper or freezer paper, be sure to place RIGHT side up of pattern onto the WRONG side of one layer of fabric. When you cut width of fabric strips for fabric shapes, be sure to cut the strip on the fold and layer fabric strips wrong side up.*

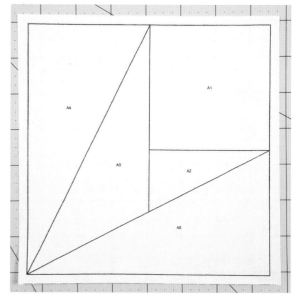

1 Using the pattern master copy, print or trace on the dull side of freezer paper or foundation paper. Trim to size leaving the seam allowance intact.

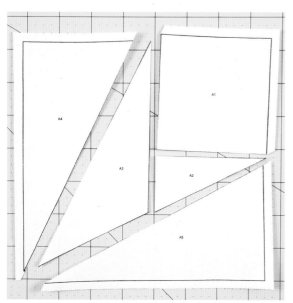

2 Cut the pattern apart on the sewing lines, leaving any seam allowance intact on the edge of the pattern. Write the pattern name or color of fabric on the paper piece to avoid a cutting error.

3 If you are using freezer paper lay the shape on the wrong side of the fabric, waxy side down, and Iron in place. Pin in place if you are using foundation paper.

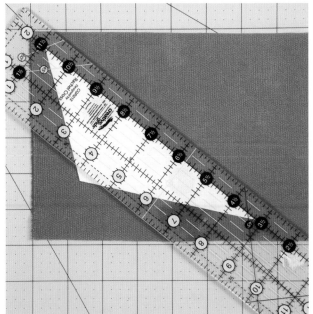

4 The photo above uses a pattern segment that has no seam allowance on any side. Make sure there is 1/2" (1.27cm) seam allowance on all sides as you cut the shape. When there is a 1/4" (0.635cm) left on a side of the pattern, add 1/4" (0.635cm) extra fabric when cutting. Use this single pattern to cut all other shapes.

Cutting Shapes from Fabric Strips

I tend to cut individual shapes for block pieces as I make them. But it's easy to cut multiple shapes. Use your patterns as they are presented in the book and cut shapes as directed. There is no need to be concerned about "mirrored" images because the block pattern takes care of it for you. (See pattern 8, page 68)

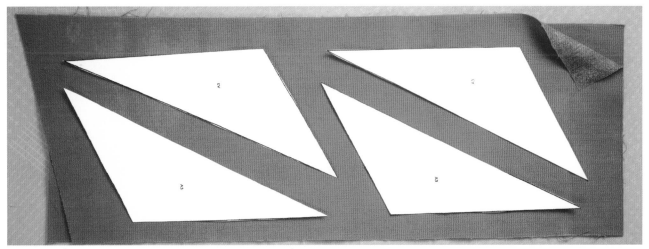

To cut more than one shape at a time, layer the fabric strips, wrong side facing up, and place pattern piece right side up. Pin in place and cut, leaving 1/2" (1.27cm) on all sides. Move the pattern across the strip to continue cutting shapes. Use your fabric efficiently by rotating pattern piece 180 degrees as you move it across the strip.

Piecing the Blocks

It's always a good idea to practice a technique before you apply it to your project. Follow this step by step once or twice and your comfort level for paper piecing with increase your skill and confidence.

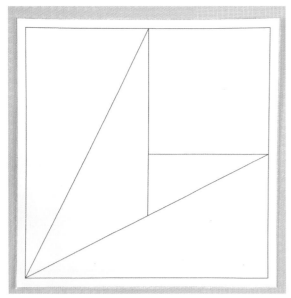

1 For this step by step, use the pattern from Starburst, page 53, to practice the paper piecing technique.

2 Cut apart one pattern on lines, leaving 1/4" (0.635cm) seam allowance intact on outer pieces. Use these pattern pieces to cut fabric shapes. (See page 8-9)

3 Use pattern pieces 1 and 2 to cut fabric shapes. Place right side of pattern on top of wrong side of fabric and pin in place. Cut around shapes leaving a 1/2" (1.27cm) around edges. If shape has 1/4" (0.635cm) line included, add only 1/4" (0.635cm) to that side.

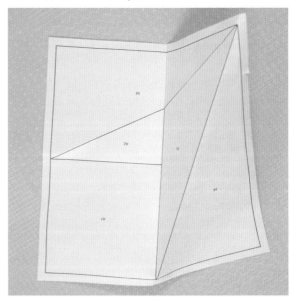

4 Crease all of the sewing lines on the pattern. This will assist in placing the fabric shapes since the fabric is placed on the back side of the pattern, the side with no lines.

Piecing the Blocks (continued)

5 Next, lay the RIGHT side of fabric shape 1 to the wrong side of paper pattern shape 1, the side with no lines. Use the fold lines as a guide and center the fabric shape as much as possible to cover the crease lines of the shape. Pin in place.

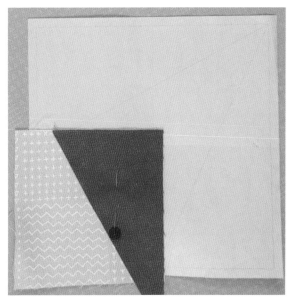

6 Layer fabric 2 onto fabric 1, right sides together, making sure the fabric overlaps the fold lines that border the shape. Pin through the fabric pieces and paper.

7 Check again to make sure the fabric shapes are overlapping the sewing lines by at least 1/4" (0.635cm). Turn pattern over and sew on the line between 1 and 2. Finish sewing 1/4" (0.635cm) past the end of the sewing line. Because the stitches are smaller, there is no need to backstitch.

8 Fold the paper on the sewn line between 1 and 2 to expose the seam allowance.

NOTE: *The extra 1/2" (1.27cm) on all sides gives you wiggle room to adjust and center fabric pieces. As long as you have a minimum of 1/4" (0.635cm) overlap on sewing line, your sewn seam will be fine.*

Piecing the Blocks (continued)

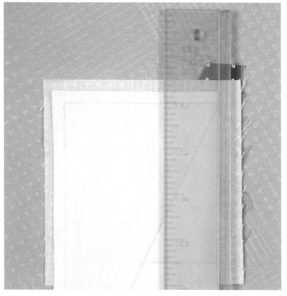

9 Trim the seam 1/4" (0.635cm) from seam line. If using an Add-A-Quarter™ ruler, (shown above) place the ridge of the ruler firmly against the seam line and trim.

10 With fabric side up, open the seam and finger press or press with an iron or wooden seam roller.

11 Cut a fabric shape for 3, leaving a 1/2" (1.27cm) around it. Lay the shape right sides together on 2, making sure the shape overlaps lines at least 1/4" (0.635cm). Pin in place.

Flip pattern to the right side of paper and sew on the line between 2 and 3.

Piecing the Blocks (continued)

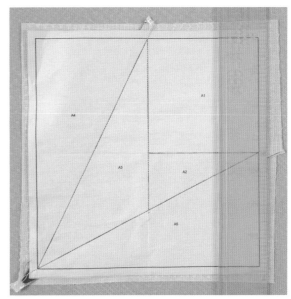

12 Fold the paper back on the sewn line to expose seam allowance. Trim 1/4" (0.635cm) from the seam.

13 Repeat steps 6-10, adding fabric shapes in numerical order until all shapes are attached. Press block and trim on the 1/4" (0.635cm) line surrounding the outside of the block.

14 Leave foundation paper intact on the completed block.

NOTE: I like to keep foundation paper attached to all my blocks until I've finished the quilt top. The extra 1/4" (0.635cm) seam serves as a guide when I'm sewing my blocks together.

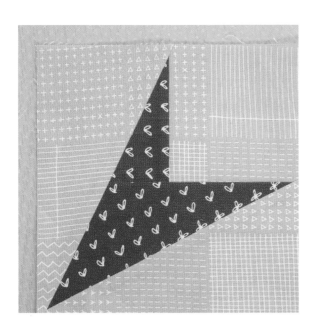

Tips

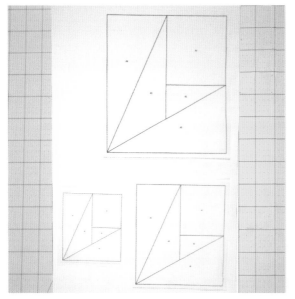

You can reduce or enlarge the patterns in this book. If you reduce, be mindful of the smallest shape in the pattern.

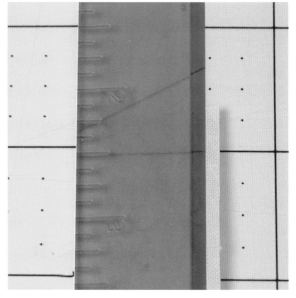

Use an Add-An-Eighth™ ruler for trimming instead of an Add-A-Quarter™ ruler to reduce bulk in smaller blocks.

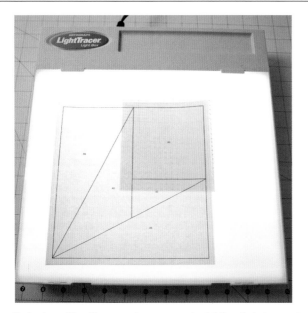

To help with alignment you can hold the fabric and paper up to a light to see the lines on the pattern. If you have a light box, it can come in handy for this step, too. Lay the fabric and paper over the box and you'll be able to check placement of your fabric shape.

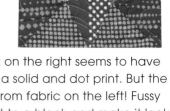

At first glance the block on the right seems to have a segment made up of a solid and dot print. But the segment was fussy cut from fabric on the left! Fussy cutting can add interest to a block and make it look far more intricate than it really is.

When you pre-cut your fabric shapes, it's a good idea to organize them, pinning the paper pattern to fabric cuts. Label a plastic bag with the name of the block and keep them bagged until you are ready to use.

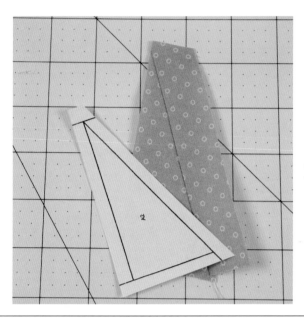

If you undercut one of your fabric shapes, and don't notice it until after you've pieced it, you have a couple of options:

1 You can use a seam ripper to remove the short piece and replace it with the correct size. If the paper rips, you can tape it back together. When removing paper from the block, take extra care when removing the tape so that stitching stays tight.

2 Or, you can add another piece of the same fabric to make the shape larger. Most people will not even notice and piecing scraps together has always been a way to create a quilt.

Which Way is Up?

Working from the front and back of a pattern can be confusing until you've paper pieced a few blocks. To ensure pieces are cut correctly, keep these tips in mind.

When cutting fabric, place pattern right side up on wrong side of fabric.

When you are ready to sew shapes together for your block, pin fabric right side up on the back of pattern shape. As you add shapes, pin fabric shapes right sides together.

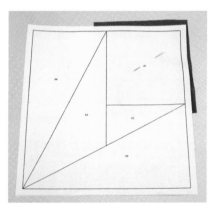

When you're ready to sew, flip the pattern over and sew on the lines.

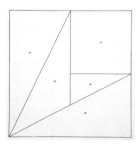

When the paper pattern on the right is removed, it reveals the seams on the back of the block. Flipping the block to the right changes the direction of the pattern. Be aware of this orientation change if a color segment needs to match a color segment in a neighboring block. The Snowflake Kaleidoscope (page 42) is a good example of the care taken when placing fabric colors that will make a continuous pattern in a quilt top.

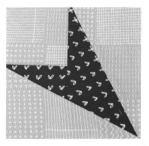

Be Loved

approximate size 64" x 64" (162.5 x 162.5cm)

Refer to the quilt photo for color inspiration. Strips in the project are cut to 2-1/4" (5.72cm) if using yardage. If jelly roll strips are used, the extra 1/4" (0.635cm) will be trimmed as you sew shapes together. Choose an assortment of reds, oranges, and pinks to outline the heart.

Materials

1-1/8 yards (102.87cm) of assorted print strips or (15) jelly roll strips for the quilt center

1-1/4 yards (102.87cm) assorted light grey print strips or (17) jelly roll strips for the border blocks

3/4 yard (68.58cm) dark charcoal solid for the quilt center blocks

3/4 yard (68.58cm) medium grey solid for the border blocks

2-3/4 yards (251.46cm) backing and batting

1/2 yard (45.72cm) binding

Copy the Pattern

For the pattern (page 52), make one master copy on office copy paper.

From the master copy print:

(43) Patterns

NOTE: *Paper piecing a project like this could just as easily be done by strip piecing. The main reason for paper piecing is the ability to make your points pointy, and make your seams match up. Because 2 out of 4 sides of each block are on the bias, the blocks can be quite stretchable, making piecing and quilting a challenge. The paper will give the blocks stability until you piece them together.*

Cutting The Fabrics

Cut apart one copy of the block pattern on the sewing lines. Leave line around the block intact.

Refer to pages 8-9, Using Patterns to Cut Fabric Shapes with foundation or freezer paper.

From assorted color strips, cut:
(10) 11" x 2-1/4" (27.9 x 5.7cm) strips
(8) 11" x 2-1/4" (27.9 x 5.7cm) various shades of red, orange and pink, or outer edge of heart
(18) 8-1/2" x 2-1/4" (21.6 x 5.7cm) strips
(18) 6-1/4" x 2-1/4" (21.6 x 5.7cm) strips
(18) 3-3/4" x 2-1/4" (9.5 x 5.7cm) strips

From assorted medium grey strips, cut:
(22) 11" x 2 -1/4" (27.9 x 5.7cm) strips
(22) 8-1/2" x 2-1/4" (21.6 x 5.7cm) strips
(22) 6-1/4" x 2-1/4" (21.6 x 5.7cm) strips
(22) 3-3/4" x 2-1/4" (9.5 x 5.7cm) strips

From dark charcoal solid, cut:
(3) 8-7/8" (22.5cm) x WOF strips. From the strips, cut:
(9) 8-7/8" (22.5cm) squares. Cut squares diagonally to make (18) triangles.
(2) 7-1/2" (19.1cm) squares

From grey solid, cut:
(3) 8-7/8" (22.5cm) strips. From the strips, cut:
(11) 8-7/8" (22.5cm) squares. Cut squares diagonally to make
(22) triangles.

Block Assembly

Refer to paper piecing instructions, page 11-13, to make 42 blocks.

Make 22   *Make 18*   *Make 2*

Quilt Assembly

1. Lay the blocks out following the Quilt Assembly Diagram below.

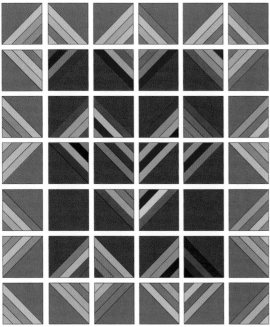

Quilt Assembly Diagram

2. Sew the blocks together in rows.

3. Sew the rows together to complete the quilt top.

Quilting Tip

For a contemporary look, quilt with clean straight lines as an allover design.

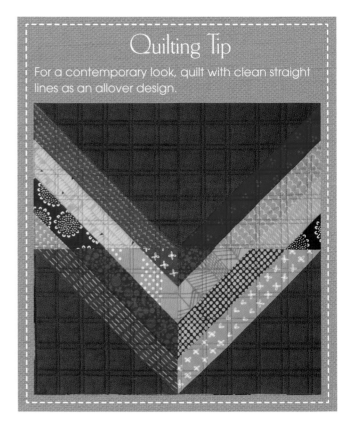

Finishing

1. Remove paper patterns from back of quilt top and press.

2. Layer the quilt top, batting and backing together. Quilt as desired.

3. Cut 2-1/2" (6.4cm) strips from binding fabric and sew together end to end to make one long binding strip. Press seams open.

4. Press strip wrong sides together. Sew to front of quilt along raw edges. Fold binding to the back, covering raw edges, and hand stitch in place.

Be Loved
64" x 64" (162.5 x 162.5cm)

Alternate Quilt

Choose a pastel palette with white triangles to create a "hidden heart". Secondary patterns abound in this color combination.

Starburst

approximate size 54" x 70" (137.1 x 177.8cm)

Materials

1/4 yard (22.86cm) cuts of 12 assorted prints for stars

4-1/2 yards (388.62cm) grey/neutral print for background, sashing and border

3-1/3 yards (304.49m) for backing and batting

2/3 yard (60.35cm) for binding

Copy the Pattern

Make one master copy of the Starburst pattern, page 53.

From the master copy print:

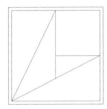

(49) Pattern 1

Cut apart one copy of the block pattern on the sewing lines. Leave line around the block intact.

Cutting The Fabrics

Refer to pages 8-9, Using Patterns to Cut Fabric Shapes with foundation or freezer paper.

From EACH of the assorted prints, cut:
(1) 4-1/2" (11.43cm) strip. Cut strip on the fold, stack wrong side up, and cut:
(4) segment 2 triangles for a total of 48

(1) 3-1/2" (7.62cm) strip. Cut strip on the fold, stack wrong side up, and cut:
(4) segment 3 triangles for a total of 48

From the grey print, cut:
From grey print, cut border and sashing pieces on the lengthwise grain.
(2) 4-1/2" x 62-1/2" (11.7 x 158.7cm) border strips
(2) 4-1/2" x 54-1/2" (11.7 x 138.4cm) border strips
(2) 2-1/2" x 62-1/2" (6.4 x 158.7cm) sashing strips
(9) 2-1/2" x 14-1/2" (6.4 x 36.8cm) sashing strips
(3) 2-1/2" (6.4cm) strips. From the strips, cut:
(9) 2-1/2" x 14-1/2" (6.4 x 36.8cm) segments
(6) 4-1/2" (11.7cm) X WOF strips. From the strips, cut:
(48) 4-1/2" squares
(12) 4-7/8" (11.7cm) strips. From the strips, cut:
(48) 4-7/8" x 9-3/4" (12.4 x 24.8cm) rectangles
Separate into 2 stacks of 24 rectangles.

From one stack cut diagonally from the LEFT to the bottom RIGHT corner to make 48 triangles.

From the remaining stack of rectangles, cut diagonally from top RIGHT corner to the bottom LEFT corner to make 48 triangles.

Block Assembly

1. Refer to Piecing the Blocks, pages 10-13. Sew 4 blocks together to make a total of 12 large blocks.

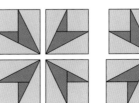 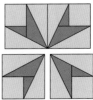 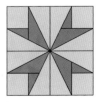

Make (12)

Quilt Assembly

1. Lay out blocks and sashing strips as shown.

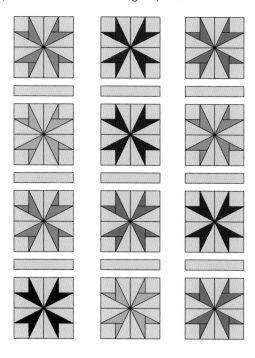

2. Sew a 2-1/2" x 14-1/2" (6.4 x 36.8cm) sashing strip to the bottom of the first block. Continue adding blocks and sashing until you have the first vertical row of 4 blocks completed. Make 2 more rows in the same manner.

3. Sew the first and second rows together with a 2-1/2" x 62-1/2" (6.4 x 158.7cm) sashing strip. Sew the second and third rows together in the same manner to finish the quilt center.

4. Sew a 4-1/2" x 62-1/2" (11.43 x 158.7cm) border to each side of the quilt center and a 4-1/2" x 54-1/2" (11.7 x 138.4cm) border to the top and bottom to complete the quilt top.

Finishing

1. Remove paper patterns from back of quilt top and press.

2. Layer the quilt top, batting and backing together. Quilt as desired.

3. Cut 2-1/2" (6.4cm) strips from binding fabric and sew together end to end to make one long binding strip. Press seams open.

4. Press strip wrong sides together. Sew to front of quilt along raw edges. Fold binding to the back, covering raw edges, and hand stitch in place.

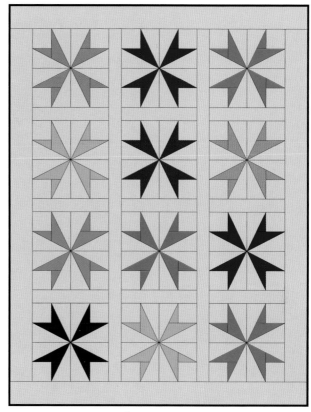

Starburst
54" x 70" (137.1 x 177.8cm)

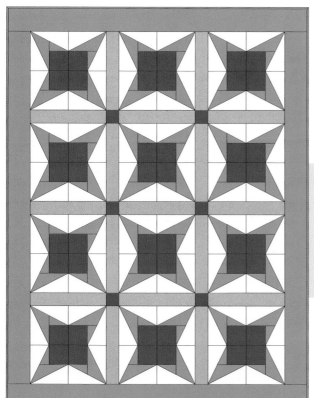

Alternate Quilt

This quilt is the same quilt with the 4 block segments rotated. The sashing, border and cornerstone are different colors. It just goes to show you how color placement and alternating block configuration can create a completely different look.

Sunday Drive

approximate size 42" x 56" (106.7 x 142.3cm)

Materials

(8) 1/4 yard (22.86cm) cuts of assorted green prints for Log Cabin Blocks

(5) 1/4 yard (22.86cm) cuts of assorted grey prints for Wonky Strip Blocks

3/4 yard (68.58cm) dark blue print
for Chevron Blocks

1-1/8 yard (102.87cm) medium blue print
for Chevron Blocks

7/8 yard (80.01cm) turquoise print
for Chevron Blocks

3-3/8 yard (308.61cm) for backing and batting

1/2 yard (45.72cm) assorted prints for binding

Copy the Patterns

For each of the patterns (pages 54-56), make one master copy on office copy paper.

From the master copies print:

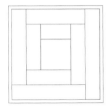

(18) Pattern 1

(19) Pattern 2

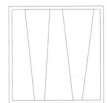

(14) Pattern 3

Cut apart one copy of each block pattern on the sewing lines. Leave line around the block intact.

Cutting The Fabrics

Refer to pages 8-9, Using Patterns to Cut Fabric Shapes with foundation or freezer paper. Keep your shapes well organized as you cut your fabric.

From assorted green prints, cut:

(2) 3-1/4" (8.3cm) strips. From the folded strips, cut:
  (17) 3-1/4" (8.3cm) center squares

(17) 2-1/2" x 3-3/8" (6.4 x 8.6cm) strips for segment 1

(34) 2-1/2" x 4-1/2" (6.4 x 11.4cm) strips for segments 2 and 3

(34) 2-1/2" x 5-5/8" (6.4 x 14.3cm) strips for segments 4 and 5

(34) 2-1/2" x 6-7/8" (6.4 x 17.5cm) strips for segments 6 and 7

(17) 2-1/2" x 7-7/8" (6.4 x 20cm) strips for segment 8

From dark blue print, cut:

(2) 4-3/4" (12.1cm) x WOF strips. From the strips, cut:
  (9) 4-3/4" (12.1cm) squares. Cut squares diagonally to make (18) triangles

(6) 2-1/2" (6.4cm) x WOF strips. From the strips, cut:
  (36) 2-1/2" x 5-7/8" (6.4 x 14.9cm) strips

From medium blue print, cut:

(6) 3" (7.6cm) x WOF strips. From the strips, cut:
  (18) 3" x 7" (7.6 x 17.8cm) segments
  (18) 3" x 5" (7.6 x 12.7cm) segments

(4) 3-3/4" (9.5cm) x WOF strips. From the strips, cut:
  (18) 3-3/4" (9.5cm) squares. Cut squares diagonally to make (36) triangles

From turquoise print, cut:

(7) 2-1/2" (6.4cm) x WOF strips. From the strips, cut:
  (18) 2-1/2" x 7-3/8" (6.4 x 18.7cm) segments
  (18) 2-1/2" x 5-7/8" (6.4 x 14.9cm) segments

From assorted grey prints:

Assign one segment shape to each of the (5) 1/4" (22.9cm) yard assorted grey prints. Pin or press pattern pieces to the *wrong side* of fabric and cut 13 shapes from each of the 5 grey prints, leaving a 1/2" (1.27cm) on all sides.

Block Assembly

Refer to Piecing the Blocks, pages 10-13 to paper piece the blocks below.

Make 17

Make 18

Make 13

Quilt Assembly

1. Complete the blocks and lay out following Quilt Assembly Diagram.

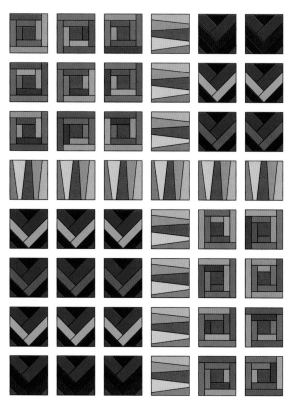

Quilt Assembly Diagram

2. Sew the blocks together in rows.

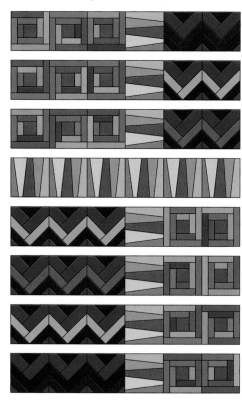

3. Sew the rows together to complete quilt top.

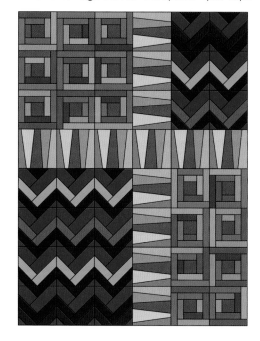

Finishing

1. Remove paper from the back of the quilt and press.

2. Layer the quilt top, batting and backing together. Quilt as desired.

3. Cut 2-1/2" (6.4cm) strips from binding fabric and sew together end to end to make one long binding strip. Press seams open.

4. Press strip wrong sides together. Sew to front of quilt along raw edges. Fold binding to the back, covering raw edges, and hand stitch in place.

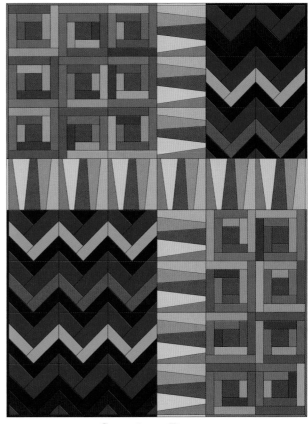

Sunday Drive
42" x 56" (106.7 x 142.3cm)

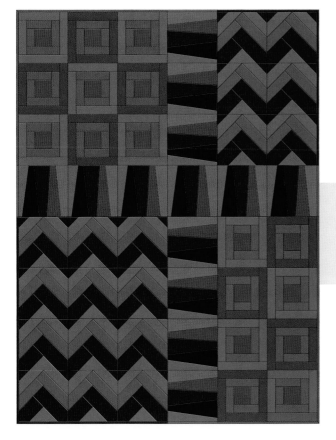

Alternate Quilt

The beautiful jewel tones in this quilt resemble gemstones. I love how color changes reinterpret the look of a quilt.

27

Supernova

approximate size 82" x 82" (208.3 x 208.3cm)

Materials

(Refer to quilt photo for color shades)

(5) 1/4 yard (22.86cm) cuts of assorted dark blue prints for star centers

(5) 1/2 yard (45.72cm) cuts of assorted turquoise prints for star points

7/8 yard (80.01cm) red/orange print for star points

1 yard (91.44cm) magenta print for stars

4-3/4 yards (434.34cm) neutral prints for background and borders

4-3/4 yards (434.34cm) for backing and batting

3/4 yard (68.58cm) for binding

Copy the Patterns

For each of the patterns (pages 57-58), make one master copy on office copy paper.

From the master copies print:

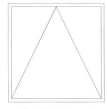

(26) Pattern 1

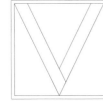

(21) Patten 2

Cut apart one copy of each block pattern on the sewing lines. Leave line around the block intact.

NOTE: *If you want to follow my colorway for each star, be sure to match colors in the different shapes within each star. This is most important with the turquoise fabric. You could buy yardage of one fun, turquoise print to make it easy!*

Cutting The Fabrics

Refer to pages 8-9, Using Patterns to Cut Fabric Shapes with foundation or freezer paper.

From EACH of the assorted dark blue prints, cut:

(1) 7-1/2" (19.3cm) square for a total of (5) star center squares

From the remainder of EACH assorted dark blue print, cut: 6-1/2" (16.5cm) X WOF strips. Leave fabric folded. Using template 1, block 2, cut:
(20) triangles

From EACH assorted turquoise print, templates 4 and 5, Block 2, cut:

(1) 8" (20.3cm) x WOF strip. From the strip, cut:
(4) left triangles for a total of 20
(4) right triangles for a total of 20

From template 1, Block 1, cut:

(4) turquoise triangles for a total of 20

From remainder of turquoise prints, cut:

(4) 7-1/2" (19.3cm) squares for a total of 20

From red/orange print fabric, cut:

(1) 1-7/8" (4.8cm) x WOF strip. Leave fabric folded and cut:
(20) 1-7/8" (4.8cm) squares for dark blue block corners

(9) 1-7/8" (4.8cm) x WOF strips. From 4 strips, cut:
(20) 1-7/8" x 7-3/4" (4.8 x 19.7cm) strips for Pattern 2, trim #2. From remaining 5 strips cut:
(20) 1-7/8" x 8-1/2" x strips for Pattern 2, trim #3

From magenta print, cut:

(3) 8" (20.3cm) x WOF strips. Using templates 2 and 3, Block 1, cut:
(16) left triangles and (16) right triangles

(1) 7-1/2" (19.1cm) x WOF strip. From strip, cut:
(4) 7-1/2" (19.1cm) squares for magenta star centers

From 1 yard (91.44cm) neutral print, cut:

(8) 3-1/2" (8.9cm) x WOF strips for borders

From 4-3/4 yards (434.34cm) assorted neutral prints, cut:

(16) 14-1/2" (36.9cm) squares

(4) 7-1/2" (19.1cm) squares

Supernova

From remainder of assorted neutral prints, cut:
8" (20.3cm) x WOF strips. Using template 1,
Block 2, cut:
(4) triangles

Using templates 2 and 3, block 2, cut:
(16) left triangles
(16) right triangles

Block Assembly

Refer to Piecing the Blocks, pages 10-13, to paper
piece the blocks below.

Make (5)
Blocks

Make (20)
Blocks

Make (4)
Squares

Make (4)
Squares

Make (12)
Blocks

Make (4)
Blocks

Make (8)
Blocks

1. Draw a line from corner to corner on (20) turquoise
7-1/2" (19.1cm) squares. Align one square on one
corner of twelve neutral 14-1/2" (36.9cm) squares.
Sew on the line and trim 1/4" (0.635cm) from the
sewn line. Press open.

Make (12)

2. Align one 7-1/2" (19.1cm) turquoise
square on opposite corners of
the remaining 4 neutral 14-1/2"
(36.9cm) squares. Sew on drawn
lines and trim 1/4" (0.635cm) from
sewn line. Press open.

Make (4)

Quilt Assembly

1. Referring to Quilt Assembly Diagram, layout blocks
as shown. Sew together in rows.

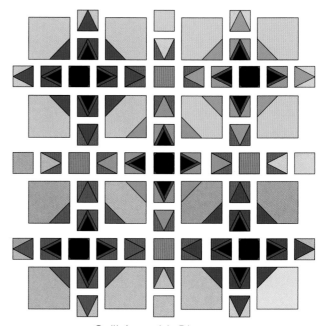

Quilt Assembly Diagram

2. Sew rows together as shown to finish quilt center.

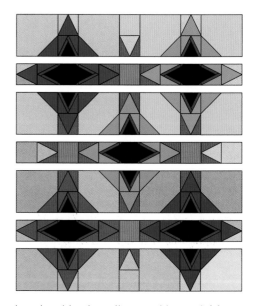

3. Sew border strips together end to end. Measure
sides of quilt top and cut borders strips to length.
Sew to each side of quilt top.

4. Measure top and bottom of quilt top and cut border strips to length. Sew to top and bottom of quilt top.

Finishing

1. Remove paper from quilt top and press.

2. Layer the quilt top, batting and backing together. Quilt as desired.

3. Cut 2-1/2" (6.4cm) strips from binding fabric and sew together, end to end, to make one long binding strip. Press seams open.

4. Press strip wrong sides together. Sew to front of quilt along raw edges. Fold binding to the back, covering raw edges, and hand stitch in place.

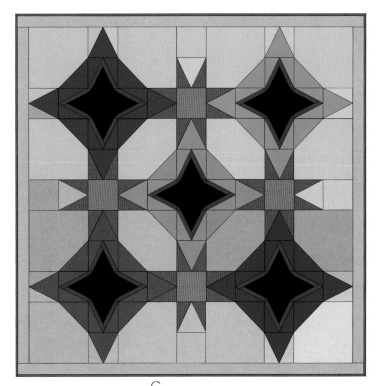

Supernova
82" x 82" (208.3 x 208.3cm)

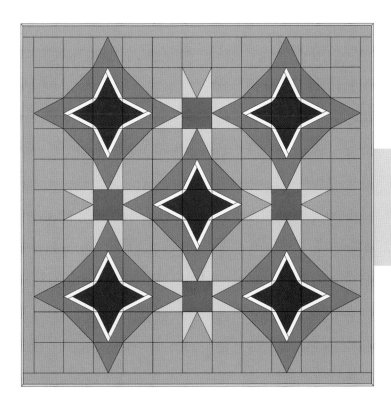

Alternate Quilt

I love the bright, exploding colors of the Supernova. But it's okay to try your own color ways, too. The quilt at left is just as striking in more subdued colors.

Sweet Tooth

approximate size 45" x 73" (114.3 x 185.4cm)

Materials

1/2 yard (45.72cm) dark grey print for star pinwheel blocks

2 yards (182.88cm) yellow/green solid for snowball blocks and small triangles in star pinwheel blocks

1 yard (91.44cm) grey/white print for large triangles in star pinwheel blocks

3/4 yard (68.58cm) rose dot print for diamonds in star pinwheel blocks

1/2 yard (45.72cm) black/white dot print for snowball blocks

1/8 yard (11.43cm) dark rose solid for diamonds and triangles in red focus blocks

1/8 yard (11.43cm) light rose solid for triangles in red focus blocks

1/3 yard (30.17cm) bright red print for red focus snowball block and small triangles in red star pinwheel blocks

1/4 yard (22.86cm) dark rose print for large triangles in red focus block

3 yards (274.32cm) for backing and batting

1/2 yard (45.72cm) for binding

Copy the Pattern

For the patterns (pages 59-60), make one master copy on office copy paper.

From the master copy print:

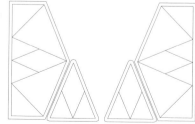

(19) each of pattern segments A, B, C and D

Cutting The Fabrics

Refer to pages 8-9, Using Patterns to Cut Fabric Shapes with foundation or freezer paper.

From dark grey print, cut:
- (4) 4-1/4" (10.8cm) x WOF strips. Using shape 5 or 7, cut: (32) 4-1/4" (10.8cm) squares. Cut squares diagonally to make (64) triangles

From yellow/green solid, cut:
- (4) 9-1/2" (24.1cm) x WOF strips. From the strips, cut: (16) 9-1/2" (24.1cm) squares
- (7) 3-1/4" (8.3cm) x WOF strips. Using shape 2 or 3, cut: (136) triangles

From grey/white print, cut:
- (5) 5-3/4" (14.6cm) x WOF strips. Using shape 4 or 6, cut: (60) triangles

From rose dot print, cut:
- (7) 2-3/4" (7cm) X WOF strips. Using shape 1, cut: (68) diamonds

From black and white dot, cut:
- (5) 3-1/8" (7.9cm) x WOF strips. From the strips, cut: (60) 3-1/8" (7.9cm) squares

From dark rose solid, cut:
- (8) 3-1/8" (7.9cm) squares for red snowball focus block and yellow/green snowball block corners
- (4) shape 1 diamonds

From the medium rose solid, cut:
- (4) 4-1/2" (11.4cm) squares. Cut squares diagonally to make (8) triangles for segments 5 and 7

From the bright red print, cut:
- (1) 9-1/2" (24.1cm) square. Using shape 2 or 3, cut: (8) triangles

From the dark rose print, cut:
- (1) 5-3/4" (14.6cm) x WOF strip. Using segment 4 or 6, cut: (12) triangles

Block Assembly

1. Draw a line from corner to corner on the 3-1/8" (7.9cm) squares. Use the illustrations below to make snowball blocks. Place a square on each block corner, right sides together, and sew on the drawn line. Trim 1/4" (0.635cm) from sewn line and press seam towards corner.

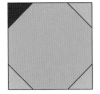 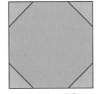

Make 4 *Make 12* *Make 1*

2. There are 4 individual segments for star block patterns. Paper piece each one following the directions on page XX and sew according to the diagram below.

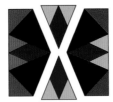

Make 14 *Make 2* *Make 2*

Quilt Assembly

1. Following the Quilt Assembly Diagram below lay out the blocks as shown.

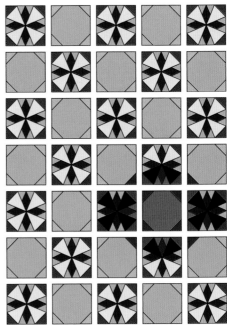

Quilt Assembly Diagram

2. Sew blocks into rows.

3. Sew rows to complete the quilt top.

Finishing

1. Remove paper patterns from back of quilt top and press.

2. Layer the quilt top, batting and backing together. Quilt as desired.

3. Cut 2-1/2" (6.4cm) strips from binding fabric and sew together, end to end, to make one long binding strip. Press seams open.

4. Press strip wrong sides together. Sew to front of quilt along raw edges. Fold binding to the back, covering raw edges, and hand stitch in place.

Sweet Tooth
45" x 63" (114.3 x 160.02cm)

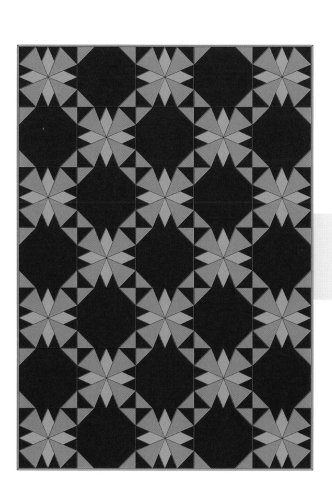

Alternate Quilt

Choosing just three colors in the contemporary brights changes the entire dynamics of the quilt.

Guess How Much I Love You

approximate size 65" x 65" (165.1 x 165.1cm)

Materials

Choose your own color values for fabrics listed below. And don't forget to dig into your stash!

4-1/2 yards (411.48cm) white for background

2-1/4 yards (205.74cm) assorted red prints

1/2 yard (45.72cm) assorted orange prints

2-1/4 yards (205.74cm) solid or a combination of assorted pink prints

1/2 yard (45.72cm) magenta print

1/2 yard (45.72cm) purple print

3-3/4 yards (342.9cm) for backing and batting

5/8 yard (57.15cm) for binding

NOTE: *Instructions for cutting fabric shapes are listed for each block. I suggest cutting fabric for each block as you make them. Use the icon for value and choose your colors accordingly.*

For the patterns (pages 61-75), make one master copy on office copy paper. Use the master to make the number of patterns for the number of blocks needed. Add an extra to use for cutting fabric shapes.

Cutting Directions

Cut apart one copy of each block pattern on the sewing lines. Leave line around the block intact.

Refer to pages 8-9, Using Patterns to Cut Fabric Shapes with foundation or freezer paper.

Block 1: Make 2 Blocks with 3 DIFFERENT colors
(1) 5-3/8" (13.7cm) x WOF strip. From the strip, cut: (4) 5-3/8" (13.7cm) squares. Cut diagonally into (8) triangles for block corners.
(1) 4" (10.2cm) x WOF strip. From the strip, cut: (4) 4" (10.2cm) squares. Cut diagonally to make (8) inner triangles.
(1) 4-1/2" (11.4cm) x WOF strip. From the strip, cut: (2) 4-1/2" (11.4cm) center squares.

Block 2: Make 2 Blocks with 3 colors
(1) 5-1/4" (13.3cm) x WOF strip. From the strip, cut: (4) 5-1/4" (13.3cm) squares. Cut diagonally to make (8) large triangles.
(1) 4-3/8" (11.1cm) x WOF strip. From the strip, cut: (4) 4-3/8" (11.1cm) squares. Cut diagonally to make (8) triangles for pinwheel.
(1) 4-3/8" (11.1cm) x WOF strip. From the strip, cut: (4) 4-3/8" (11.1cm) squares. Cut diagonally to make (8) triangles for pinwheel.

Block 3: Make 2 Blocks with 5 colors
(2) 2-3/4" (7cm) center squares.
(1) 3" (7.6cm) x WOF strip. From the strip, cut: (4) 3" (7.6cm) squares. Cut diagonally to make (2) each of 2, 3, 4, and 5 triangles.
(1) 3-5/8" (9.2cm) x WOF strip. From the strip, cut: (4) 3-5/8" (9.2cm) squares. Cut diagonally to make (2) each of 6, 7, 8, and 9 triangles.
(1) 4-1/8" (10.5cm) x WOF strip. From the strip, cut: (4) 4-1/8" (10.5cm) squares. Cut diagonally to make (2) each of 10, 11, 12, and13 triangles.
(1) 5-1/4" (13.3cm) x WOF strip. From the strip, cut: (4) 5-1/4" (13.3cm) squares. Cut diagonally to make (2) each of 14, 15, 16 and 17 triangles.

Block 4: Make 4 Blocks with 5 DIFFERENT colors

NOTE: *Use one pattern for all triangles.*

(1) 4" (10.2cm) x WOF strip from 5 assorted colors.

(6) 4" (10.2cm) squares. Cut diagonally to make (12) triangles.

(4) 4" (10.2cm) squares. Cut diagonally to make (8) triangles.

(4) 4" (10.2cm) squares. Cut diagonally to make (8) triangles.

(2) 4" (10.2cm) squares. Cut diagonally to make (4) triangles

(2) 4" (10.2cm) squares. Cut diagonally to make (4) triangles.

Block 5: Make 2 Blocks with 2 colors

(1) 3-3/4" (9.5cm) x WOF strip. Cut the strip on the fold line and stack wrong sides facing up. Use shape 1or 6 and cut a total of (8) shapes.

(1) 3-1/2" (8.9cm) x WOF strip. Cut the strip on the fold line and stack wrong sides facing up. Use shape 3 or 4 and cut a total of (8) shapes.

(1) 2" (5.1cm) x WOF strip. Cut the strip on the fold line and stack wrong sides facing up. Use shape 2 or 5 and cut a total of (8) shapes.

Block 6: Make 2 Blocks with 4 colors

(1) 3-1/4" (8.3cm) x WOF strip. From the strip, cut: (2) A1 and (2) C1 shapes.

(1) 3-1/4" (8.3cm) x WOF strip. From the strip, cut: (2) B1 and (2) D1 shapes.

Note: *in this block, these shapes were fussy cut from a fabric print. See page 14*

(1) 3-3/4" (9.5cm) x WOF strip (2) of each of the following A2, A3, C2, and C3.

(1) 3-3/4" (9.5cm) x WOF strip. (2) of each of the following: B2, B3, D2, and D3.

Block 7: Make 1 Block with 5 colors

(1) 6"(15.2cm) x WOF strip, and cut: 1 each of shapes 1A, B, C, D and 3A, B, C, and D

From remaining 4 colors, and matching the sets, cut:

(1) 3" x 9-1/2" (7.6 x 24.1cm) strip. From the strip, cut:
(1) A2 and B4
(1) B2 and C4,
(1) C2 and D4,
(1) D2 and A4

Block 8: Make 2 Blocks with 4 colors

Match color of lettered/numbered shapes A/B 2, A/B 4 A/B 6.

(2) 3" (7.6cm) x WOF strips. Cut and stack strips wrong sides up. From strips cut:
(2) each of shapes A1, 3, 5, 7 and B1, 3, 5, 7.

(1) 3" x 16-1/4" (7.6 x 41.3cm) strip. With fabric wrong side up, cut:
(2) A2 and (2) B2 shapes.

(1) 3" x 13-1/2" (7.6 x 34.3cm) strip. With fabric wrong side up, cut:
(2) A4 and (2) B4 shapes.

(1) 3" x 8" (7.6 x 20.3cm) strip. With fabric wrong side up, cut:
(2) A6 and (2) B6 shapes.

Block 9: Make 1 Block with 4 colors

Choose 2 bright colors for the center pinwheel.

(1) 2-1/4" x 16" (5.715 x 40.6cm) strip, and cut:
(1) each of A1, C1, E1, and G1

(1) 2-1/4" x 16" (5.715 x 40.6cm) strip, and cut:
(1) each of B1, D1, F1, and H1

(1) 1-3/4" (4.5cm) x WOF strip and cut:
(1) each of shape 3, A, C, E, and G
(1) each of shape 3 B, D, F, and H

(1) 2-7/8" (7.3cm) x WOF strip and cut:
(1) each of shape 2 A, C, E, and G
(1) each of shape 2 B, D, F, and H
(1) each of shape 4 A, C, E, and G
(1) each of shape 4 B, D, F, and H

Block 10: Make 1 Block with 3 colors

(1) 3-1/8" (7.9cm) x WOF, and cut:
(1) each of shape 2, A-H

(1) 2" (5.08cm) x WOF, and cut:
(1) each of shape 4, A-H

(1) 3-1/8" (7.9cm) x WOF, and cut:
(1) each of shape 1 A, C, E, and G
(1) each of shape 1 B, D, F, and H
(1) each of shape 3 A, C, E, and G

Block 11: Make 2 Blocks with 5 colors

(1) 2" (5.08cm) x WOF strip. From the strip, cut:
(2) each of shape 1 A and C, and
(2) each of E and G

(1) 2" (5.08cm) x WOF strip. From the strip, cut:
(2) each of shape 1 B and D, and
(2) each of F and H

(1) 3" (7.6cm) x WOF strip. From the strip, cut:
(2) each of shape 2 A and C, and
(2) each of E and G

(1) 3" (7.6cm) x WOF strip. From the strip, cut:
(2) each of shape 2 B and D, and
(2) each of F and H

(1) 2-3/4" (7.cm) x WOF strip. From the strip, cut:
(2) each of shape 3 A,C, E and G
(2) each of shape 3 B,D, F and H, and

(1) 2-1/2" (6.35cm) x WOF strip. From the strip, cut:
(2) each of shape 3 A, C, E and G
(2) each of shape 3 B,D, F and H, and
(1)1-7/8" 4.8cm) x WOF strip. From
the strip, cut:
(2) each of shape 4 A,C, E
and G (2) each of shape 4 B,D, F and H.

Block 12: Make 68 Blocks in three colors

From white fabric, cut:
(5) 4-7/8" (12.382cm) X WOF strips.
From the strips, cut:
(36) 4-7/8" (12.382cm) squares. Cut squares
twice diagonally to make
(144) triangles.

From second color cut:
(5) 2-1/2" (6.4cm) X WOF strips.
From the strips, cut:
(68) 2-1/2" (6.4cm) squares

From third color, cut:
(21) 1-1/2" (3.8cm) X WOF strips.
From **6** strips, cut:
(68) 1-1/2" x 3-1/2" (3.8 x 8.9cm) strips
From **10** strips, cut:
(136) 1-1/2" x 3" (3.8 x 7.6cm) strips
From **5** strips, cut:
(68) 1-1/2" x 2-1/2" (3.8 x 6.4cm) strips

Quilt Background
From white fabric, cut:

(1) 20-1/2" (52.1cm) square. Cut
diagonally to make 2 half-square
triangles, one for either side of
heart bottom.

(1) 5-5/8" (14.3cm) square.
Cut diagonally to make
(2) half-square triangles for either side
of heart top.

(1) 7-1/2" (19.1cm) square. Cut square
diagonally and use 1 triangle for
center of heart.

(2) 8-1/2" x 54-1/4" (21.6 x 138.8cm) strips
for inner side borders

(1) 13-1/4" x 38-5/8" (33.7 x 98.1cm) strip
for top inner border

(1) 8-3/4" x 38-5/8" (22.2 x 98.1cm) strip
for bottom inner border

(4) 2-3/4" x 65-3/4" (7 x 167.0cm)
outer borders

Block Assembly

1. Refer to pages 10-13 Piecing the
Blocks. Press finished blocks, leaving
paper pattern attached.

2. For each of block !, sew a small white half-square triangle to either side of each block as shown.

3. Sew block 12 to make 68 border units. Sew border units together to make (2) 16 unit strips and (2) 18 unit strips. Use extra triangles to square up the strips as shown.

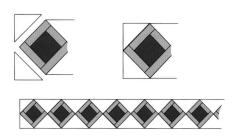

Quilt Assembly

1. Lay out blocks as shown. Sew blocks in diagonal rows. Sew the rows to complete the heart.

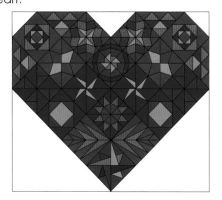

2. Sew a large half-square triangle to each side of the heart. Trim to square up if necessary. Press quilt center and remove paper patterns from back of heart.

3. Sew the 13-1/4" x 40" (33.65 x101.6cm) strip to top of heart.

4. Sew the 9-1/4" x 40" (23.495 x101.6cm) strip to bottom of heart.

5. Sew the 8-3/4" x 56-1/2" (22.22 x 143.51cm) strips to each side of heart.

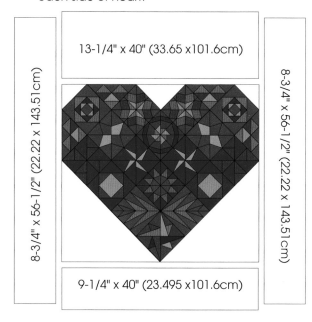

6. Sew a 16 unit pieced border to top and bottom of quilt.

7. Sew an 18 unit pieced border to eah side of the quilt.

8. Sew a 2" (5.08cm) outer border strip to each side of quilt and trim if necessary.

9. Sew a 2" (5.08cm) outer border strip to top and bottom of quilt and trim if necessary.

Finishing

1. Remove paper patterns from back of quilt top and press.

2. Layer the quilt top, batting and backing together. Quilt as desired.

3. Cut 2-1/2" (6.4cm) strips from binding fabric and sew together, end to end, to make one long binding strip. Press seams open.

4. Press strip wrong sides together. Sew to front of quilt along raw edges. Fold binding to the back, covering raw edges, and hand stitch in place.

Guess How Much I Love You
66" x 66" (167.64 x 167.64cm)

Alternate Quilt

Choose one block and make 17 identical blocks to create the heart. Remember to make the 1/2 block for the top and sides of the heart.

Snowflake Kaleidoscope

approximate size 60" x 80" (152.5 x 203.2cm)

Materials

2-3/4 yards (251.46cm) red prints

1/2 yard (45.72cm) dark red print

1 yard (91.44cm) rich red print

3 yards (274.32cm) white prints

1-1/8 yards (102.87cm) green prints

2-1/4 yards (205.74m) blue prints

5/8 yard (57.15cm) rose red print

1/4 yard (22.86cm) bright red prints

4-5/8 yard (422.91cm) batting and batting

5/8 yard (57.15cm) binding

Copy the Pattern

For the pattern (pages 76-78), make one master copy on office copy paper.

From the master copy print:

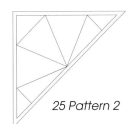

25 Pattern 2

85 Pattern 1

5 Pattern 3

Before You Start...

I designed this quilt starting with the center block. Working in rounds, I chose my colors as I sewed the blocks from one round to the next.

I used Kaffe Fassett fabrics, which are very colorful and extremely patterned. As long as you choose the same values in the reds, blues and greens, you can recreate the "feel" of this quilt.

But, your fabric choices can be whatever colors are your favorites. Be sure to buy yardage amounts as directed in the materials list using your choice of colors. Keep in mind that prints will give you a variety of values and textures.

No strips are required to cut shapes. Cut and piece the number of shapes you need for the blocks in each round. Total blocks needed for each round are provided.

Use your fabric efficiently as you place patterns and cut around shapes. If pieces are small, like the corner triangles, you may have fabric in your stash that will work well.

This is a challenging quilt but if you take the time to "build as you go", I have no doubt you'll be successful.

As You Build, Remember...

Because you add fabric on the wrong side of the pattern, your completed fabric block will be reversed from the orientation of the paper pattern.

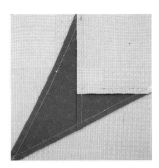 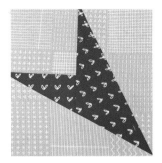

On the left, the paper with sewing lines has been removed to reveal the seams. On the right, the finished block is now reversed from the paper pattern.

Snowflake Kaleidoscope

As you start to build your quilt, refer to the illustration on page 46 to determine color choices that will recreate the patterns within the quilt top.

Pay close attention to the paper pattern pieces. You can see in the blocks below how triangles appear and disappear.

In the opposite corners of the third block below, the pattern segments were cut as diamonds and the diamonds in opposite corners were cut as 2 triangles. Refer to the illustrated blocks in each round and pay close attention as you cut shapes.

Round 1

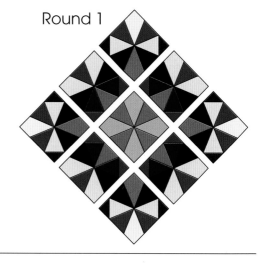

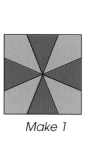

Make 1

Make 4

Make 4

Round 2

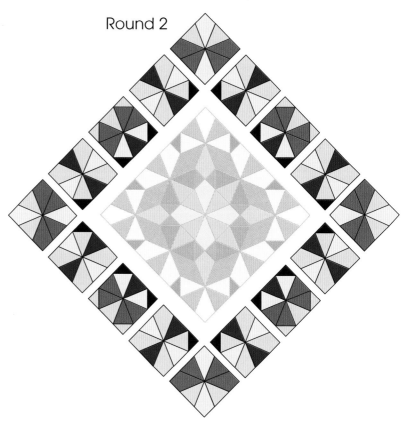

Make 4

Make 4

Make 4 of each

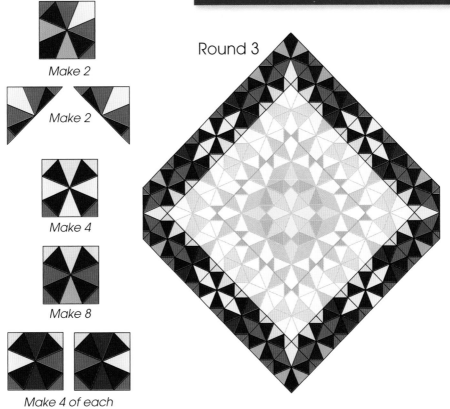

Make 2

Make 2

Make 4

Make 8

Make 4 of each

Round 3

Round 4

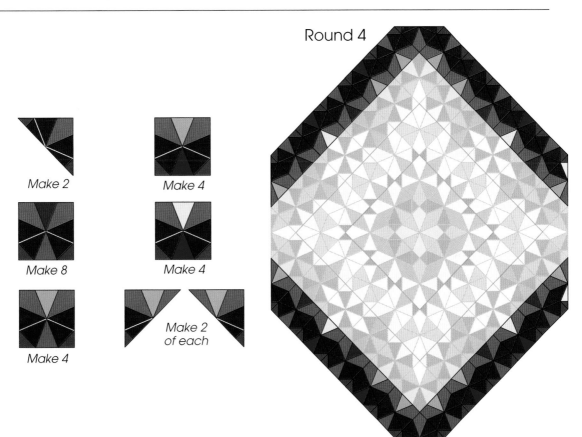

Make 2

Make 4

Make 8

Make 4

Make 4

Make 2 of each

 *Make 4 of each* *Make 8* *Make 4*

 Make 4 *Make 4 of each*

Round 5

Round 6

Round 7

  Make 4

Finishing

1. Remove paper patterns from back of quilt and press.

2. Layer the quilt top, batting and backing together. Quilt as desired.

3. Cut 2-1/2" (6.4cm) strips from binding fabric and sew together, end to end, to make one long binding strip. Press seams open.

4. Press strip wrong sides together. Sew to front of quilt along raw edges. Fold binding to the back, covering raw edges, and hand stitch in place.

Snowflake Kaleidoscope
60" x 80" (152.5 x 203.2cm)

Alternate Quilt

The same blocks and layout, are used in this version of the Snowflake Kaleidoscope. Using only four colors creates more clarity in the block and the movement of the quilt is quite dramatic in solids.

Diamond in the Rough

approximate size 44" x 57" (111.8 x 144.8cm)

Materials

For Shape 1:
(1) 3/8 yard (34.29cm) cut from **EACH** of dark blue print, turquoise print, red print, and brick print

(1) 3/8 yard (34.29cm) cut from **EACH** of 3 assorted yellow prints

For Shape 2:
Note: Coordinate medium and dark colors for small center diamonds
(5) 1/8 yard (11.43cm) cuts of medium solid for Shape 2A

(5) 1/8 yard (11.43cm) cuts of dark solid for shape 2B

For Shape 3:
3/8 yard (34.29cm) light grey solid for shape 3A
3/8 yard (34.29cm) white solid for shape 3B

For Shape 4:
3/8 yard (34.29cm) dark grey solid for Shape 4A

3/8 yard (34.29m) black solid for Shape 4B

(3) 1/3 yard (30.17cm) cuts of assorted light prints for border triangles

3-1/2 yards (320.04cm) backing and batting

1/2 yard (0.50m) for binding

Copy the Pattern

For the pattern (pages 79-80), make one master copy on office copy paper.

From the master copy print:

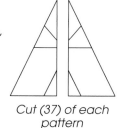

Cut (37) of each pattern

Cutting The Fabrics

Cut apart one copy of the block pattern on the sewing lines. Leave line around the block intact.

Refer to pages 8-9, Using Patterns to Cut Fabric Shapes with foundation or freezer paper.

NOTE: *There are two paper triangle templates for this project, A and B. They are mirrored images of each other. Be mindful when organizing your fabrics, keeping A and B pattern segments separate.*

Shape 1
From EACH 3/8 yd (34.29cm) cut of dark blue, turquoise, red and brick print, cut:
(2) 5-3/4" (14.6cm) x WOF strips. Cut strips on the fold and stack fabric wrong side up, and cut:
     (6) A1 shapes for a total of 24
     (6) B1 shapes for a total of 24

From EACH 3/8 yd (34.29cm) cut of assorted yellow fabrics, cut:
(2) 5-3/4" (14.6cm) x WOF strips. Cut strips on the fold and stack fabric wrong sides up, and cut:
     (4) A1 shapes for a total of 12
     (4) B1 shapes for a total of 12

Shape 2
For this shape, you need a total of (36) A2 and (36) B2 shapes.

Coordinate A2 and B2 medium and dark colors for each of the center diamonds in the quilt. (Refer to quilt photo) Use your fabric colors in whatever way complements your fabric for A1 and B1 shapes.

Shape 3
From white and light grey solids, cut:
(2) 3-1/2" (8.9cm) x WOF strips. From the strips, cut:
     (36) 3A white shapes
     (36) 3B light grey shapes

From dark grey and black solids, cut:
(2) 5" (12.7cm) x WOF strips. From the strips, cut:
     (36) 4A dark grey shapes
     (36) 4B black shapes

Border Triangles (leave fabric cuts folded)

From 1/3 yard (30.17cm) assorted light print cuts, cut:

(12) 10-7/8" x 6-1/4" (27.6 x 15.9cm) rectangles.
Cut rectangles into 2 triangles for a total of
(12) left triangles and (12) right triangles.

Block Assembly

1 Refer to paper piecing instructions, page 10-13, for
block assembly. Because of the mirrored images,
this would be a good time to use a design wall to
lay out your blocks.

Quilt Assembly Diagram

2. Sew the segments together to create rows.

Quilt Assembly:

Sew the rows together to complete the quilt top.
Remove paper from back of top.

Quilting Tip

Straight line quilting is one the easiest quilting
techniques for beginner's to successfully finish a
modern quilt.

Finishing

1. Remove paper patterns from back of quilt and press.

2. Layer the quilt top, batting and backing together. Quilt as desired.

3. Cut 2-1/2" (6.4cm) strips from binding fabric and sew together end to end to make one long binding strip. Press seams open.

4. Press strip wrong sides together. Sew to front of quilt along raw edges. Fold binding to the back, covering raw edges, and hand stitch in place.

Diamond in the Rough
44" x 57" (111.8 x 144.8cm)

Alternate Quilt

By limiting your color choices you can create a much calmer quilt. Secondary patterns are easier to see in this colorway.

Enlarge 110%

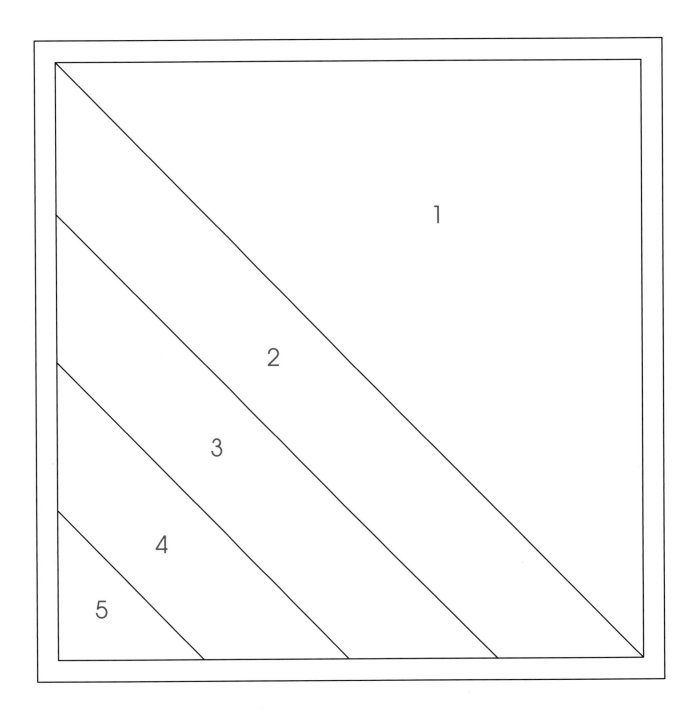

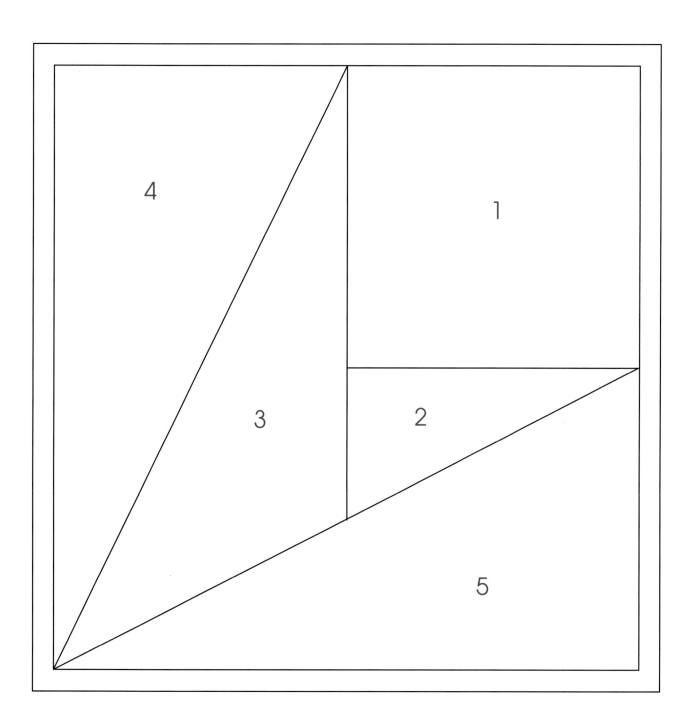

Sunday Drive Pattern 1

Enlarge 110%

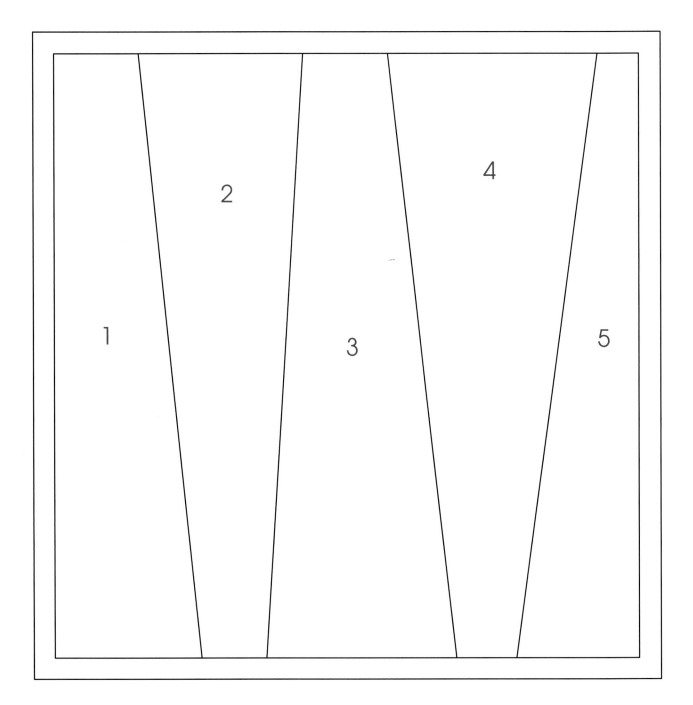

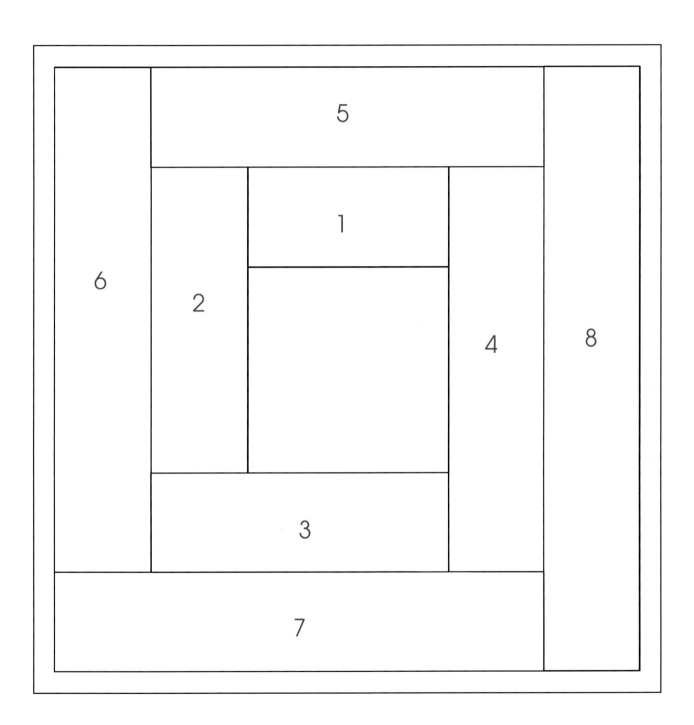

Sunday Drive Pattern 3

Enlarge 110%

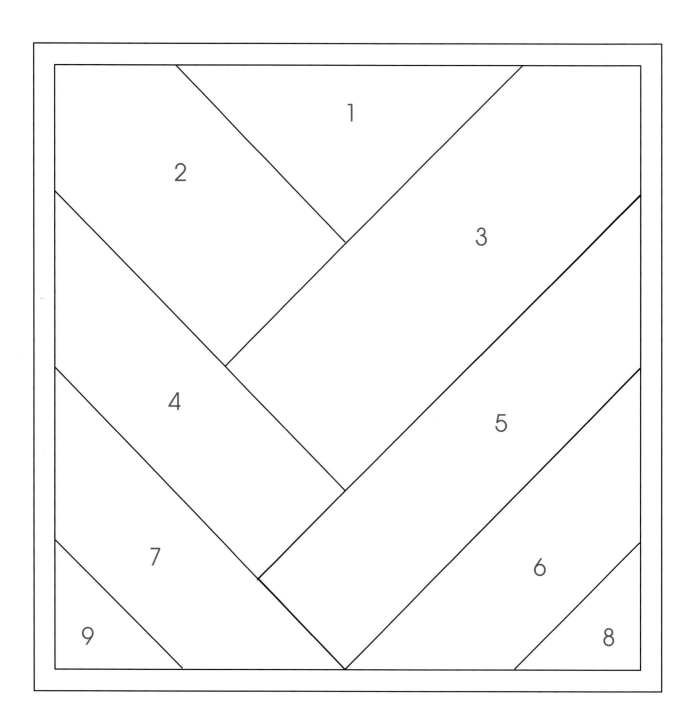

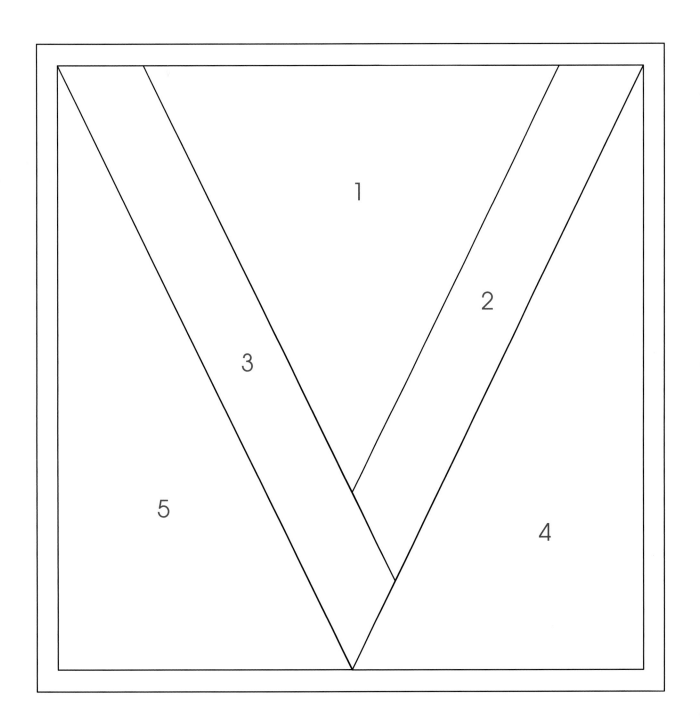

Supernova Pattern 2

Enlarge 110%

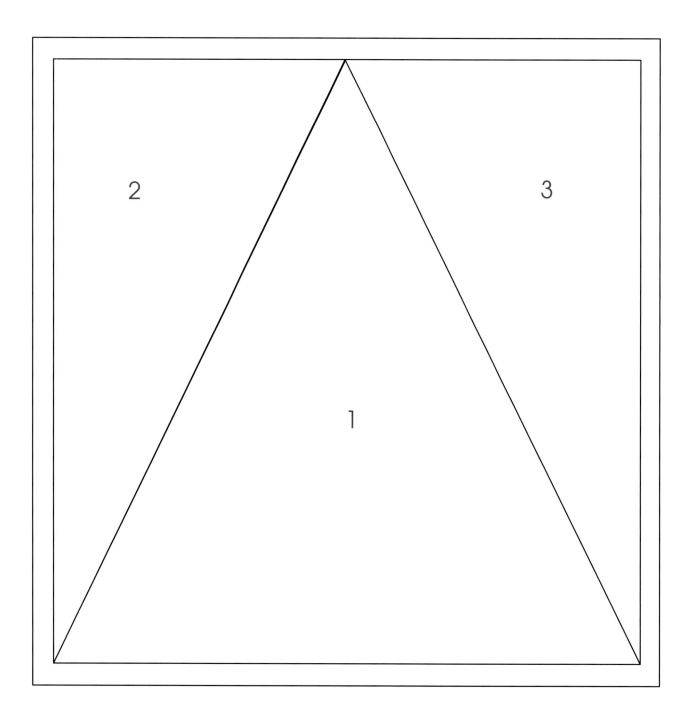

Enlarge 110%

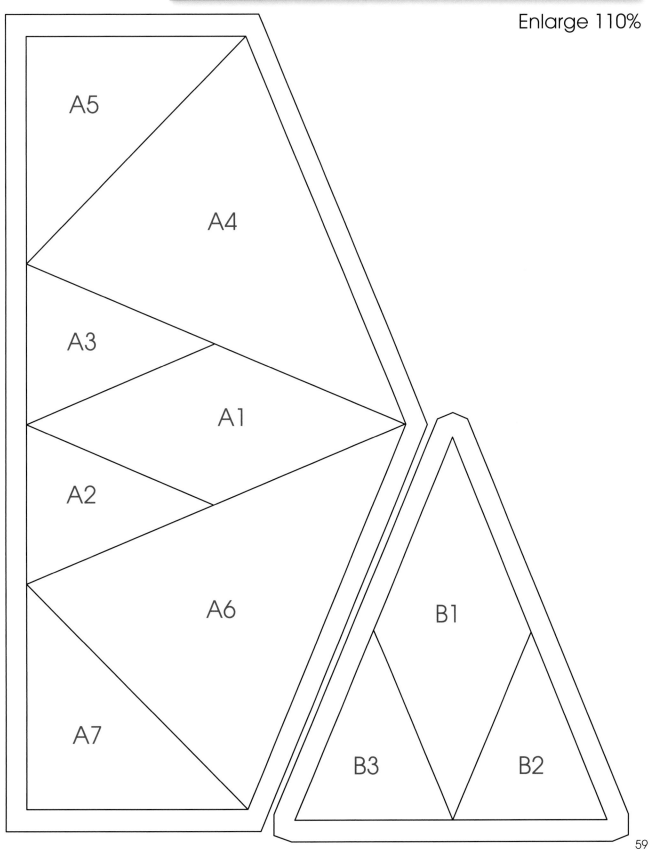

Enlarge 110%

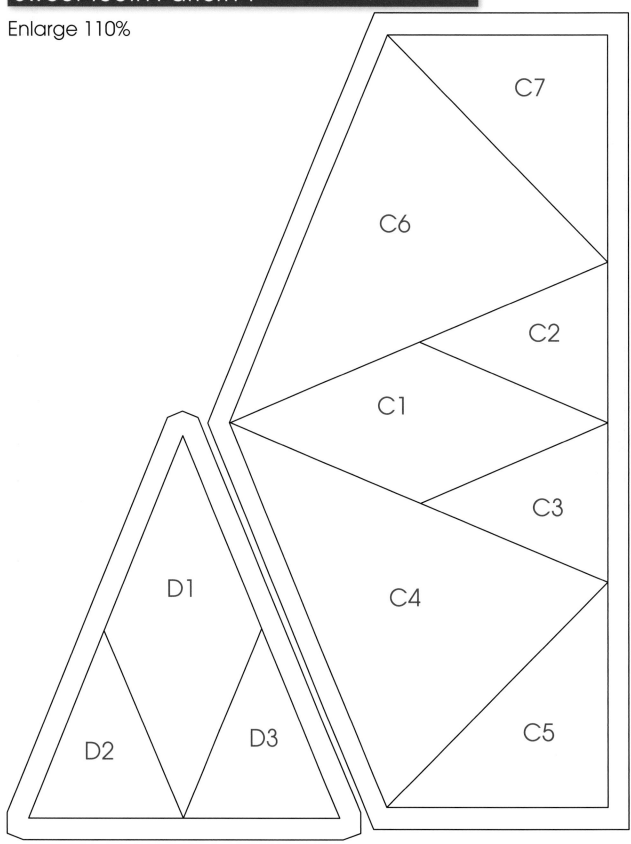

Enlarge 110%

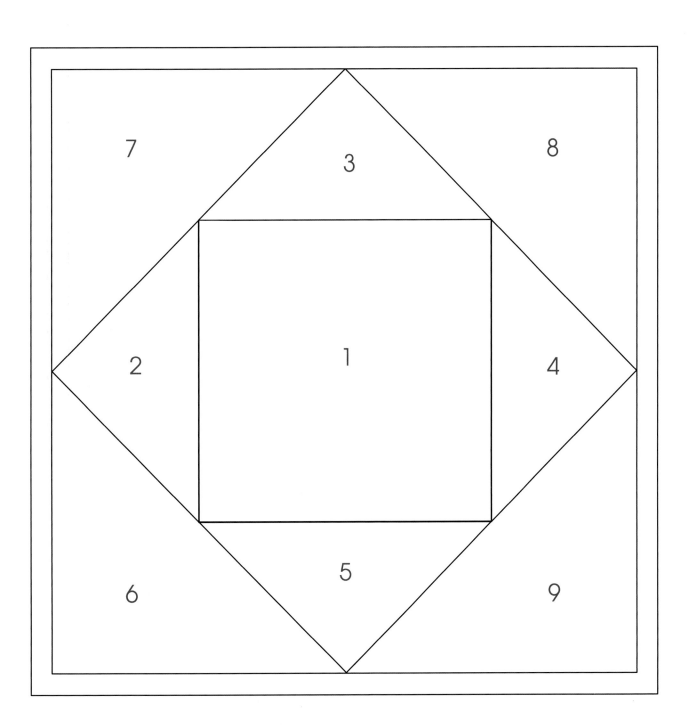

Enlarge 110%

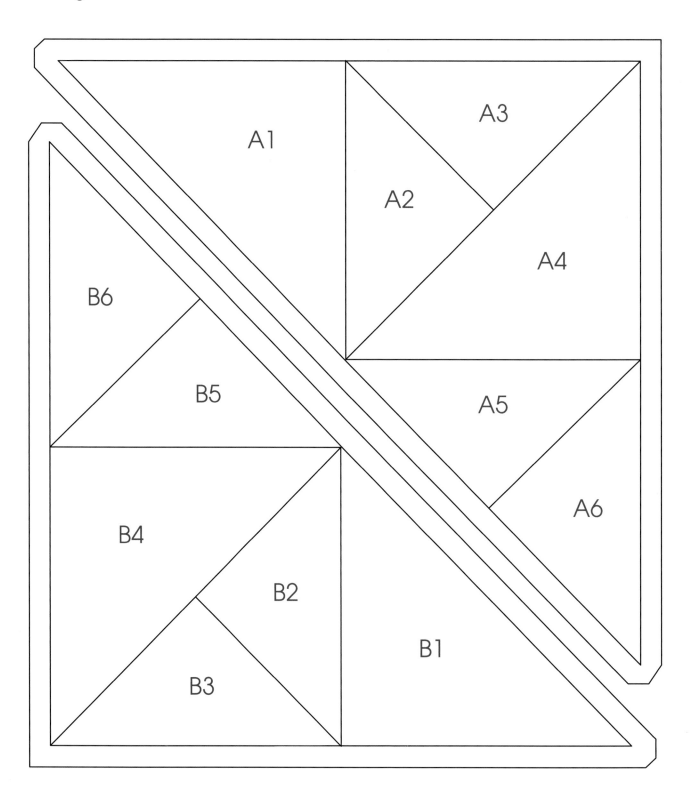

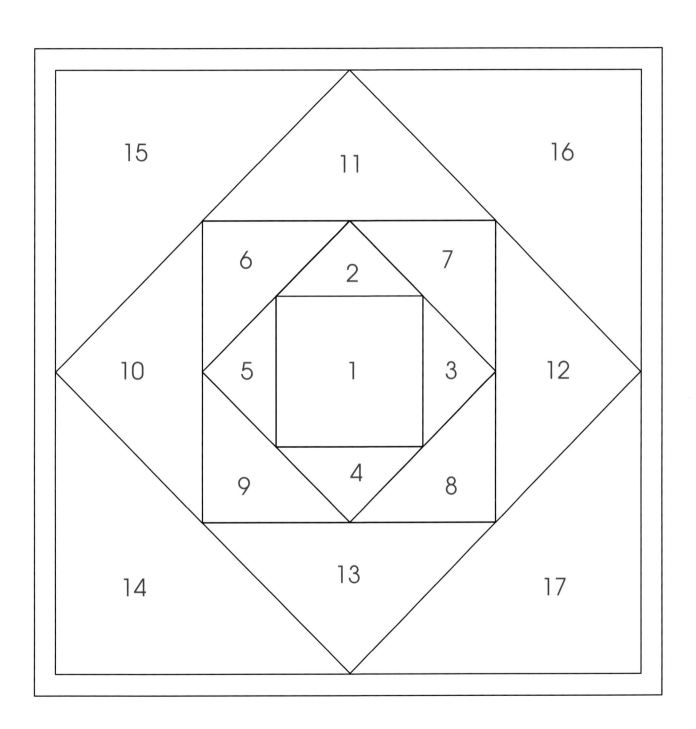

Enlarge 110%

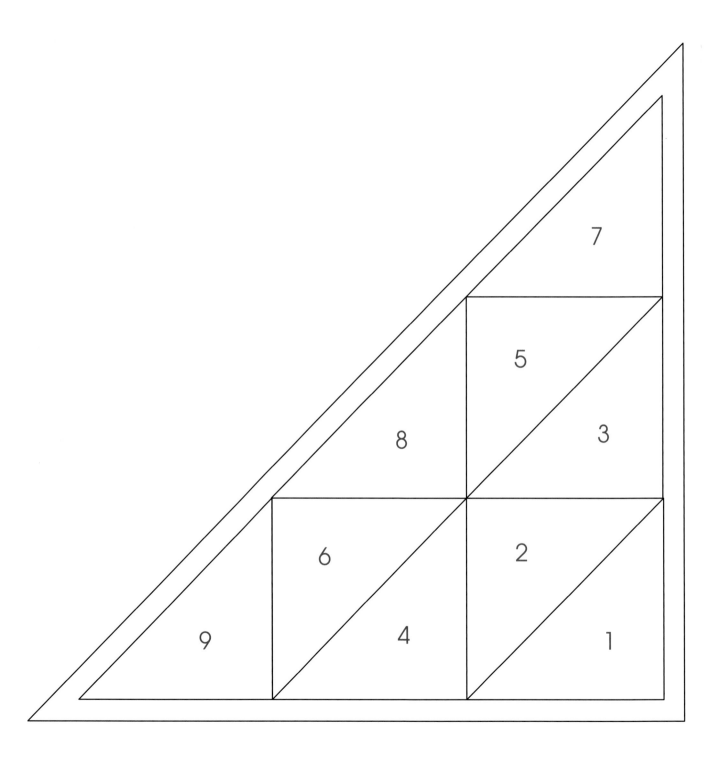

Enlarge 110%

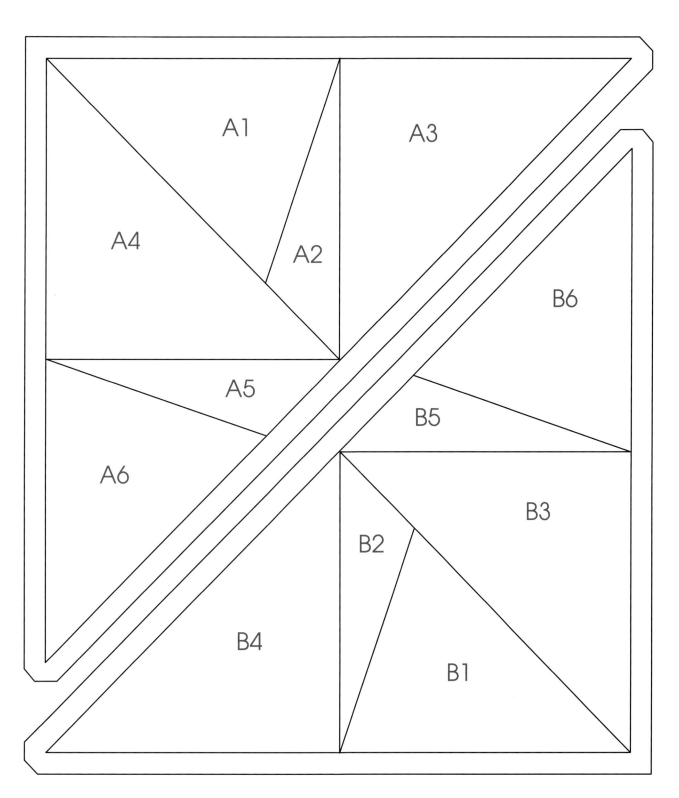

Enlarge 110%

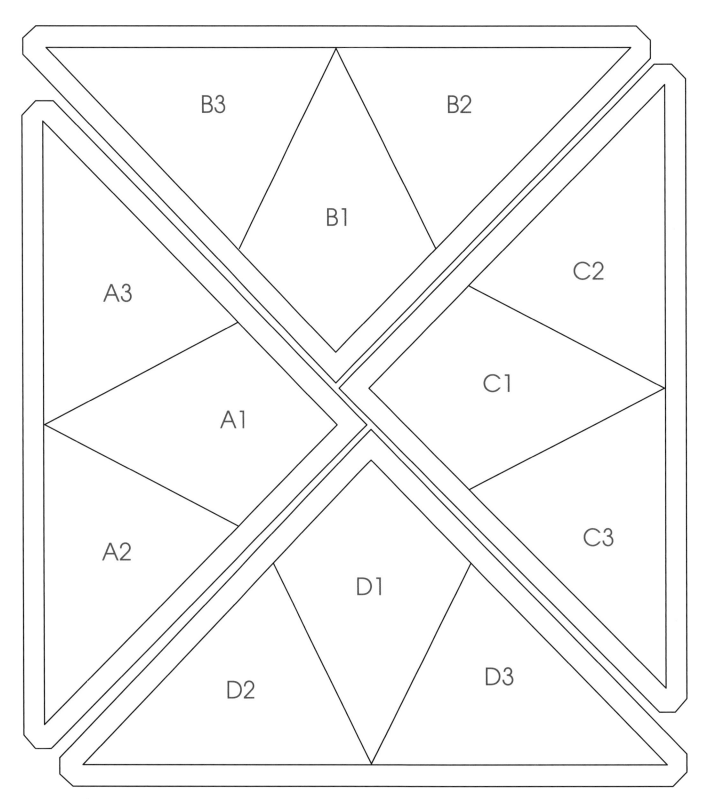

Enlarge 110%

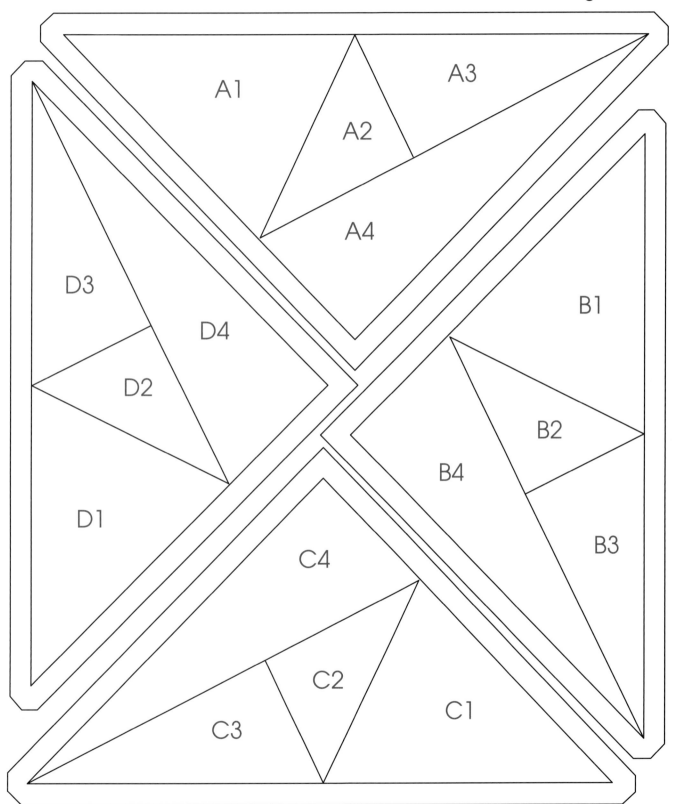

Enlarge 110%

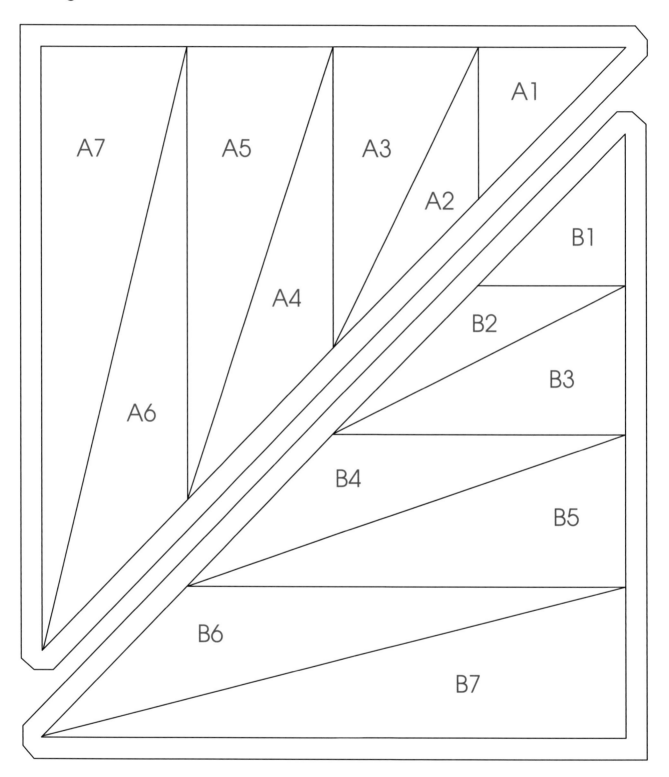

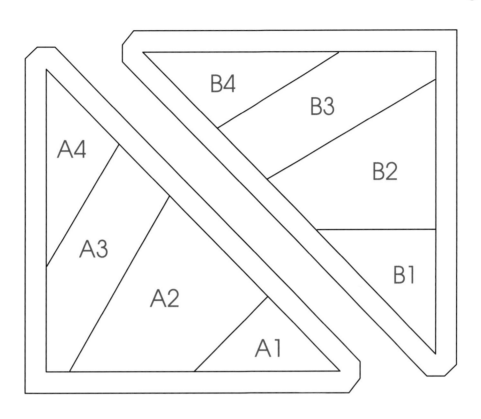

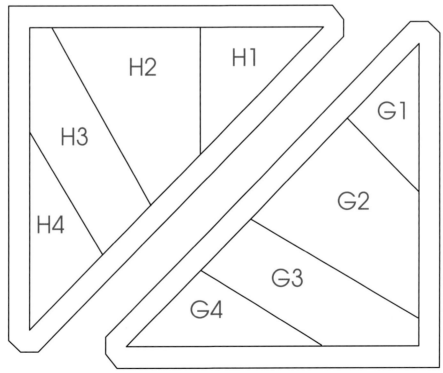

Enlarge 110%

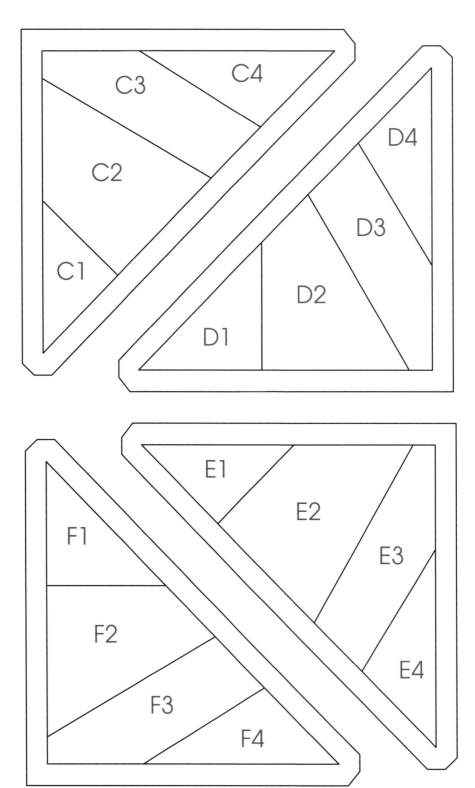

Enlarge 110%

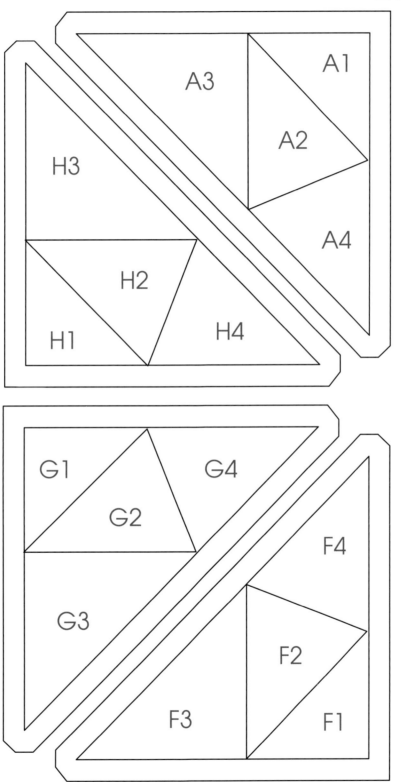

Enlarge 110%

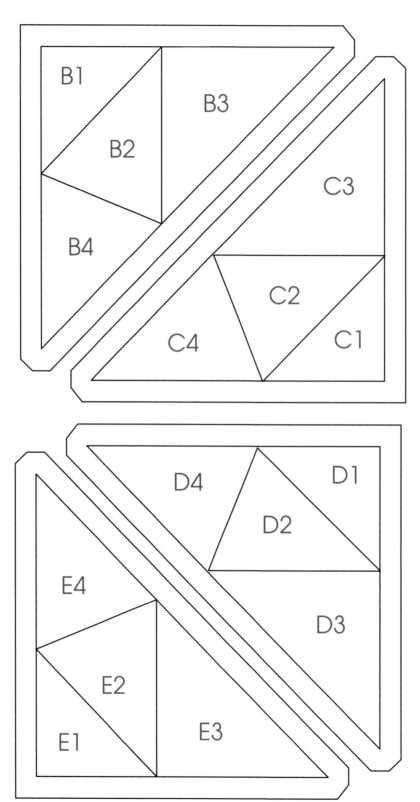

Enlarge 110%

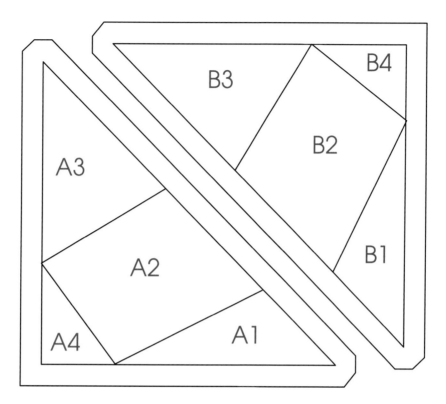

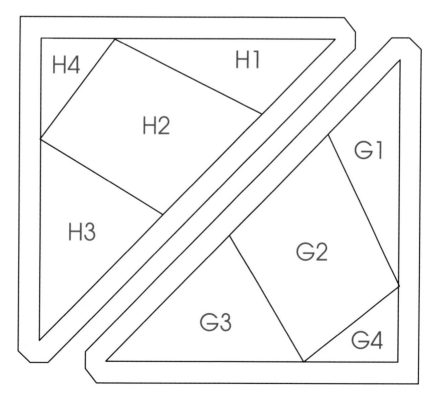

Enlarge 110%

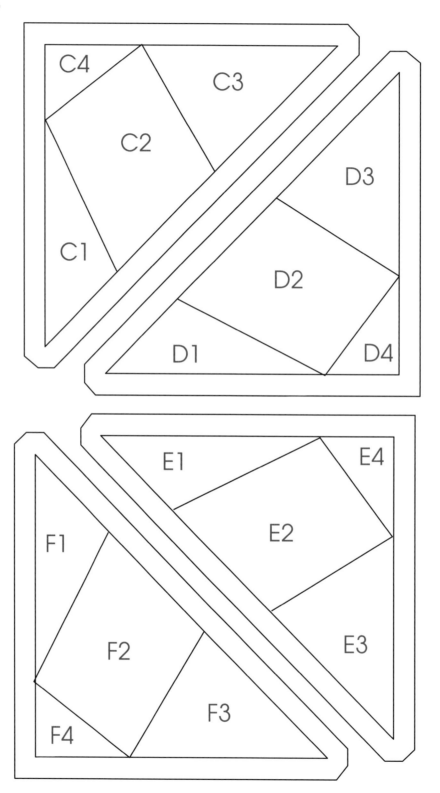

Enlarge 110%

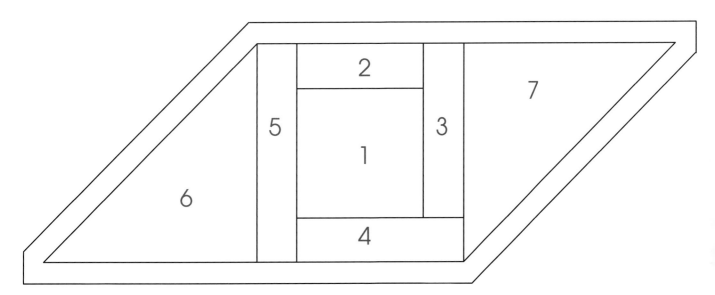

Snowflake Kaleidoscope Pattern 1

Enlarge 110%

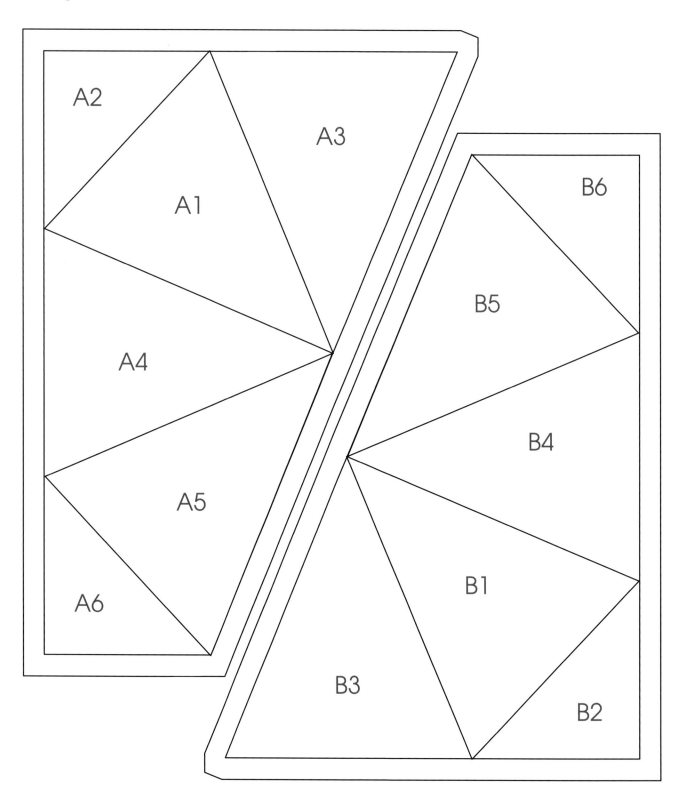

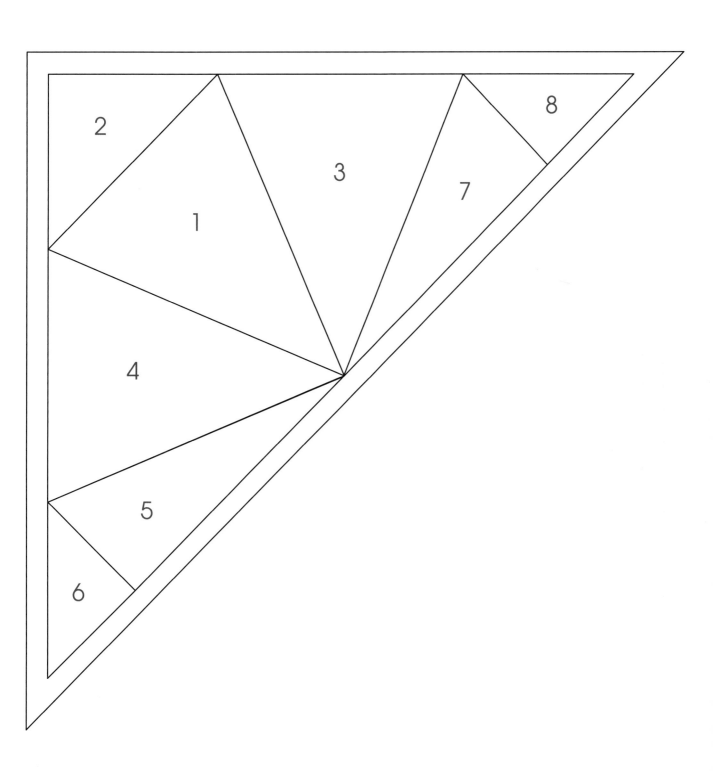

Snowflake Kaleidoscope Pattern 3

Enlarge 110%

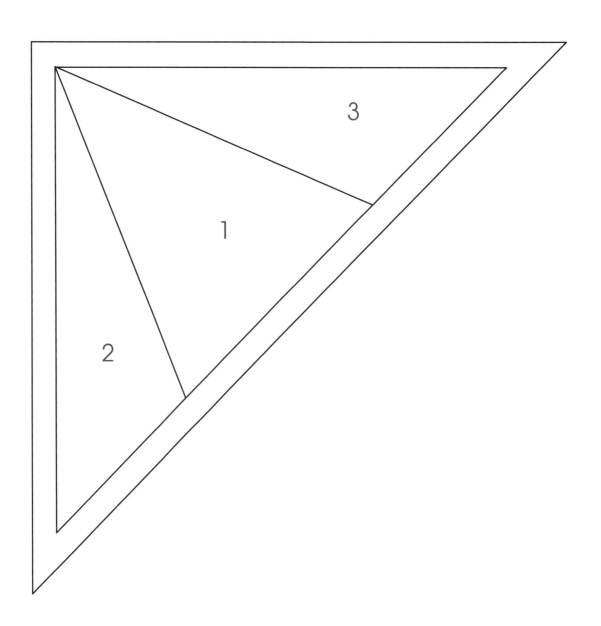

Enlarge 110%

A2

A1

A3

A4

Enlarge 110%

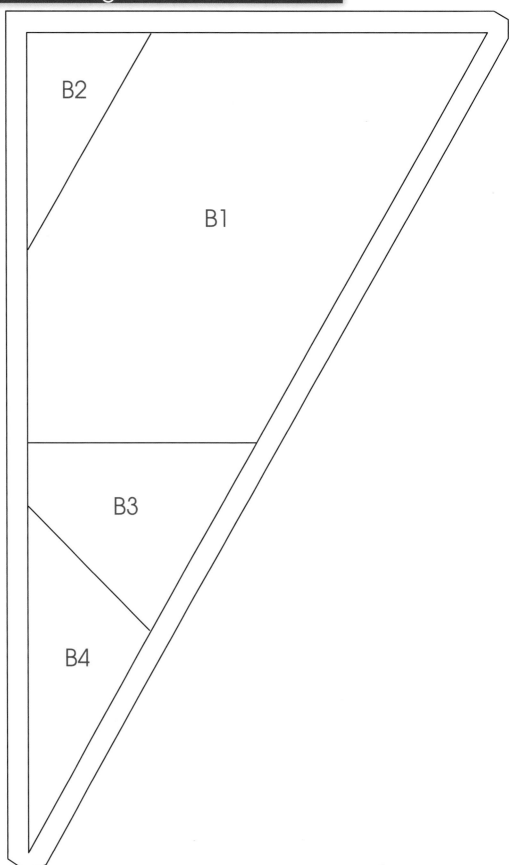